The Project Manager's Toolkit

The Project Manager's Toolkit
Practical Checklists for Systems Development

David M. Shailer

Routledge
Taylor & Francis Group

LONDON AND NEW YORK

First published by Butterworth-Heinemann

First published 2001

This edition published 2011 by Routledge
2 Park Square, Milton Park, Abingdon, Oxon OX14 4RN
711 Third Avenue, New York, NY 10017, USA

Routledge is an imprint of the Taylor & Francis Group, an informa business

British Library Cataloguing in Publication Data
A catalogue record for this book is available from the British Library

ISBN 0 7506 5035 4

Contents

Computer Weekly Professional Series

There are few professions which require as much continuous updating as that of the IS executive. Not only does the hardware and software scene change relentlessly, but also ideas about the actual management of the IS function are being continuously modified, updated and changed. Thus keeping abreast of what is going on is really a major task.

Computer Weekly Professional Series has been created to assist IT executives keep up-to-date with the management ideas and issues of which they need to be aware.

One of the key objectives of the series is to reduce the time it takes for leading edge management ideas to move from academic and consulting environments into the hands of the IT practitioner. Thus, this series employs appropriate technology to speed up the publishing process. Where appropriate some books are supported by CD-ROM or by additional information or templates located on the Web.

This series provides IT professionals with an opportunity to build up a bookcase of easily accessible but detailed information on the important issues that they need to be aware of to successfully perform their jobs as they move into the new millennium.

Aspiring or already established authors are invited to get in touch with me if they would like to be published in this series.

Dr Dan Remenyi, Series Editor
Dan.remenyi@mcil.co.uk

Series Editor
Dan Remenyi, MCIL

Series Advisory Board
Frank Bannister, Trinity College Dublin
Ross Bentley, Management Editor, *Computer Weekly*
Egon Berghout, Technical University of Delft
Ann Brown, City University Business School
Roger Clark, The Australian National University
Reet Cronk, University of Southern Queensland

Arthur Money, Henley Management College
Sue Nugus, MCIL
David Taylor, CERTUS
Terry White, BentleyWest, Johannesburg

Series titles published

IT investment – Making a business case
The effective measurement and management of IT costs and benefits
Stop IT project failures through risk management
Understanding the Internet
Prince 2: A practical handbook
Considering computer contracting?
David Taylor's Inside Track
A hacker's guide to project management
Corporate politics for IT managers: how to get streetwise
Subnet design for efficient networks
Information warfare: Corporate attack and defence in a digital world

Preface

This book was nearly titled *The Joy of Checks* but fortunately I was persuaded otherwise before I got too fond of it. But I do find using checks and checklists a joy. Checklists are a very powerful way to control IT tasks because they are:

- easy to follow
- don't rely on memory so things don't get forgotten
- can be refined or augmented
- can be produced and agreed upon in a team context.

This book contains varieties of checklists to show how useful they can be. This variety is to enable project managers or lead-analysts to dip into the book to find a checklist that covers a particular problem or need rather than have to read the whole book cover to cover.

Within the book, there are three basic types of checklist:

- **To do** – can be used as a method to do something.
- **Analysis** – normally raise questions that have to be answered in your own context; they may or may not give some clues as to how to deal with what you find.
- **QA** – can be used to check a deliverable.

There aren't strict demarcations between the types of checklists. For example, a QA checklist can be used as a definition of what needs to be done (i.e. as a To do list). But they give some idea of what to expect within the checklist and how to apply them.

Finally, the checklists don't cover every situation. They have to be applied wisely and tailored to your own needs and environment. They may need to be reduced, augmented or changed as circumstances demand. If you have any comments/additions/amendments about these or your own checklists, please email me on toolkit@accompli.co.uk.

Acknowledgements

The main input to this book has been from notes collected over the years from a variety of sources – magazine articles, seminars, memos, conversations with colleagues etc. – too numerous to list. Hence I would like to thank all those who have wittingly or unwittingly contributed to this book.

Also I would particularly like to thank Geoff Quentin (QCC) and Stuart Dinnen for their inspired use of checklists in the past. It was through their vision that I captured my notes to create checklists for myself.

1
Project inception checklists

1.1 Getting the project kick-off meeting right

Type: To do

Checklist description

Major projects often start with project kick-off meetings. These meetings set the tone of the project and are the point where all interested parties are brought up to the same level of understanding about what the project is intended to achieve and how it is intended to run.

This is a simple checklist to indicate what should be covered in the project kick-off meeting – effectively, the meeting's agenda. It goes without saying that it is very important that all interested parties be invited to the meeting.

Checklist

1   Describe the project background (see checklist 1.2 'Five key areas to understand when starting a project').

2   Outline the project objectives and goals (see checklist 1.3 'Dealing with hidden agendas – where to start'). Explicitly state the goals.
  (a) Primary goals:
      (i)   To achieve what? Specific benefits with numbers, volumes, rates (e.g. 25 per cent more query calls handled per day)
      (ii) By when?
      (iii) At what cost?
      (iv) For the benefit of whom?
      (v)   Giving them what benefits?
  (b) Secondary goals:
      (i)   Using whom?
      (ii) With what additional benefits (e.g. new skills, PR value, higher morale etc.)?

3   Set scope of project and expectations.

4   Show milestones and plan.

5   Show individuals their part and reporting lines.

6   Outline what standards are to be used.

7   Outline project controls – status reporting, timesheets, change control, configuration control.

Definitions/techniques

None.

Next steps

It should be clear from the above that project kick-off meetings don't just happen. A great deal of project work needs to occur prior to the meeting as indicated by the relevant checklists. It is recommended that this background work be conducted prior to the meeting rather than after it – there is nothing so demoralizing on a project than a lack of confidence in the project and business management. That lack of confidence is easy to engender – just go to a project kick-off meeting where there is tension between the project manager and the business managers to see what I mean.

With a good project meeting in the bag, people will want to start work so it's best not to hold such a meeting when there is going to be a gap (no matter how small) between the meeting and starting project work. Ideally the project plan should contain some early, simple, small-win tasks that can be started immediately and finished within the month. This will continue the 'feel-good' factor on the project – nothing breeds success like success.

1.2 Five key areas to understand when starting a project

Type: Analysis

Checklist description

'It's not how you start, it's how you finish' may sound good in a Hollywood musical but, in IT projects, how you start often determines whether you finish at all. One of the important building blocks of a project is to understand where it fits in the organization – its context.

The following checklist is relevant whether the project is new or whether you are new to the project. Using the checklist will help you to plot the course for what to do next, what is important or unimportant and who your customers are.

Checklist

1   Understand the IT strategy:
    (a)   Does the organization have an IT strategy?
    (b)   How old/applicable is it?
    (c)   Who are the owners of the strategy?
    (d)   What is the corporate vision and is the IT strategy backed up by the corporate vision?
    (e)   What are the short-, medium-, long-term goals of the strategy?
    (f)   Which parts of the organization are affected by the strategy and are they currently in a state of change?
    (g)   What external parties are affected by the strategy – suppliers, customers, unions, professional/trade bodies?
    (h)   What are the benefits to the organization, departments and individuals of the strategy?

2   Understand where this project stands in terms of the IT strategy:
    (a)   What contribution will this project make to the overall strategy?
    (b)   Why now?
    (c)   Who is the beneficiary of the project? Have they approved the project?
    (d)   Who are the main contributors to the project's success? Do they know of the project and are they committed to its success? Is there any conflict between the contributors regarding the project?
    (e)   What departments will be directly or indirectly affected by this project?
    (f)   To what extent will they be impacted?
    (g)   Who are the main influencers in these departments?
    (h)   What level of planning and acceptance will be required from the main influencers?
    (i)   What are the impacts on external parties of this project and to what extent are actions required to involve these parties?

3   Check the commitment of the project sponsor:
    (a)   Is the currently allocated project sponsor appropriate to this project? Are they a major stakeholder in the benefit of the project?
    (b)   Do they have ultimate responsibility for budget, timescale, acceptance criteria, sign-off?
    (c)   Has the project sponsor stated the benefits to be achieved – what are they?
    (d)   What priority has the project sponsor given this project above his/her own activities?

(e) Is it clear from the project sponsor that this is a worthwhile project that has to be tackled now?

4 Understand what limits and constraints have been imposed:

(a) What has been specified as a given on:
   (i) hardware
   (ii) software
   (iii) timescale
   (iv) delivery date
   (v) resources
   (vi) budget
   (vii) scope.

(b) Are the limits reasonable given the objectives? Are you allowed to challenge the limits?

(c) What are the deliverables? Are they agreed? Has the quality of them been agreed?

(d) Do project milestones exist? What are they? What happens if you don't meet them? Are they reasonable given the quality requirements?

(e) Is there anything required before the project can begin – office space, machines/IT, personnel? What is the timescale for getting these items? Is there sufficient budget for getting these items?

5 Understand the project's history:

(a) What work has already been done? Is it available? Is it to standard and quality? Is there anything missing which will have to be done under the new project's auspices?

(b) Who has been involved up to now? What is their role? Is their role continuing? Have responsibilities been assigned? Who to and for what? Are the demarcations clear? Are they reasonable? Are handover points identified along with the level of quality expected at each handover point?

Definitions/techniques

None.

Next steps

The answers to the above questions should be captured in a section in a Project Charter or Project Handbook. This can be given to individuals assigned to the project to help them understand the project's context in the organization.

With this information in place, it is now time to start the task of project 'start-up' – see checklist 1.1 'Getting the project kick-off meeting right'.

Note that the project goals and objectives are especially important to get right at the start of the project and hence a separate checklist has been included to examine this aspect more closely.

1.3 Dealing with hidden agendas – where to start

Type: Analysis

Checklist description

Even at the start of a project, some work has already been done. It could be just some ideas in the MD's head or minutes from a board meeting four months ago. However it happened, senior management have started to have expectations of the project. The objectives of the project, the project boundaries, and the way the project is expected to progress are gradually being set in their mind's eye.

Without a formal agreement on the project's objectives it is highly likely that each individual will have framed the project slightly differently. It's also possible that individuals' objectives are now incompatible with each other.

With all this work going on, it's critical to get formal agreement about the nature of the project. This checklist is useful for driving out what the project's objectives and boundaries are. Naturally, more than one person should be used as the source of this information and if inconsistencies arise, a formal meeting to resolve issues can be conducted.

Checklist

1   What level of business process change is expected?

☐ Full business process redesign – an IT solution may or may not be required subsequently.

☐ Business process is to be automated as currently defined with additional process-improvement functions.

☐ Business process is to be automated as currently defined, i.e. system must fit around the business process.

☐ Business process can be tailored to fit in with system but not fundamentally changed, i.e. business will fit around the system to a degree.

☐ Undetermined – will take recommendations.

2   What type of IT system is envisaged?

☐ Full bespoke development.

☐ Package system to be selected and implemented.

☐ Package system to be selected, tailored and implemented.

☐ Hybrid of package and bespoke development.

☐ Undetermined – will take recommendations.

3   What type of project process is thought most suitable?

☐ Prototyping – evolutionary/incremental.

☐ Formal development/package selection process.

☐ Mixture of prototyping and formal process.

☐ Undetermined – will take recommendations.

4   What elements of the project can be reviewed?

▢ Can the project be assessed against the current business policy? Can the project objectives be changed?

▢ Can the current business policy be assessed against the project? Can the policy be changed?

▢ What alternatives have been considered to deliver the business benefits? Can additional alternatives be proffered?

▢ What limits have been set against the project (e.g. budget, timescale, resources, quality)? Can these be changed?

Definitions/techniques

Types of prototyping:

• Evolutionary – each version of the prototype is fully functional in its own right.
• Incremental – each version of the prototype is partly functional until the whole system is built.

Next steps

Naturally, it's best to gather this information first before forming a conclusion. The outcome of the above (once formally consistent and agreed) will determine what activities to include in the planning exercise (see checklist 1.6 'Determining the big three – targets, timescales and budgets'). Another option would be to consider conducting a risk assessment on the information gleaned thus far – see checklist 1.4 'How to do a simple risk assessment'.

A useful by-product of this analysis is to consider whether it is better to separate the business analysis activities from the systems development process, i.e. set up two projects rather than one. Quite often, until the business analysis has been conducted, it is difficult to determine the size and scope of the system-development project. Hence it is better not to set deadlines or estimates on this second project upfront. This gives business managers an opportunity or second chance to evaluate what is being done and how much it will cost without being committed to it.

Another checklist that examines some of the project assumptions is 1.2 'Five key areas to understand when starting a project'.

1.4 How to do a simple risk assessment

Type: To do

Checklist description

There are many ways to assess the risk of a project to a company, e.g. SWOT analysis. The following scoring system is only one method. The scorings can be added to suit your organization and project. Especially interesting to include are any factors that have caused problems on previous projects.

Checklist

Score the project as follows:

(a) New application is:
    (i)   new   = 3
    (ii) mixture of new and old   = 2
    (iii) rehash of old   = 1

(b) Project manager is:
    (i)   new   = 3
    (ii) 2–4 years' experience   = 2
    (iii) old hand   = 1

(c) Project is expected to last:
    (i)   more than 12 months   = 3
    (ii) more than 6 months   = 2
    (iii) up to 6 months   = 1

(d) Number of departments involved:
    (i)   more than 3   = 3
    (ii) 2–3   = 2
    (iii) only one   = 1

(e) The application area is:
    (i)   new to the team   = 3
    (ii) new to some of the team   = 2
    (iii) old to most of the team   = 1

(f) The team individuals are:
    (i)   new to one another   = 3
    (ii) new to some   = 2
    (iii) old work colleagues   = 1

(g) The budget is set:
    (i)   independently (e.g. the board)   = 3
    (ii) project sponsor   = 2
    (iii) sponsor and project manager   = 1

(h) The timescale is set:
    (i)   independently (e.g. the board)   = 3
    (ii) project sponsor   = 2
    (iii) sponsor and project manager   = 1

(i) The board-level support is:
    (i)   low (leaving it to sponsor) $= 3$
    (ii)   some (want progress reports) $= 2$
    (iii) high (want to be involved) $= 1$

(j) The interfaces are:
    (i)   to external systems $= 3$
    (ii)   to internal systems $= 2$
    (iii) none – standalone $= 1$

Factor these responses for a final total by using the factors shown in the formula below for each letter:

- Total $= 5a + 5b + 3c + 5d + 4e + 3f + 5g + 5h + 5i + 4j$.
- Interpret your result according to these bands: 44–$66 =$ low risk, 67–$112 =$ medium risk, 113–$132 =$ high risk.

Definitions/techniques

SWOT – a brainstorming technique to list the attributes of a project in terms of Strengths/ Weaknesses, Opportunities/Threats. By dividing up the project into opposing quadrants it can be seen (visually) whether the strengths/opportunities outweigh the weaknesses/threats.

Next steps

Where a project has some high-risk elements, further work is required to determine how to bring down the score for some or all of the values marked as 3. Risk-management strategies may include:

- training
- team building
- presentation and buy-in strategies
- renegotiation of project scope (e.g. scope difficult functions into a separate project)
- use of outside (experienced) resources.

These actions would need to be added to the project plan – see checklist 1.6 'Determining the big three – targets, timescales and budgets'.

1.5 Twelve project procedures to have in place before you start

Type: QA

Checklist description

The very fact that projects need project managers indicates that projects need management procedures with structures and rules. A good project manager can ease his/her own burden by putting in place various policies, procedures and practices. It will ease his/her own burden since people can follow these procedures without needing the project manager to advise thus leaving the project manager to deal with problems and issues rather than the routine.

The rule is: **get organized now** (because there won't be time later). The more procedures in place, the smoother the running of the project (although there is a need to avoid being overbureaucratic).

This checklist gives a project manager an idea of the procedures that should be in place before a project starts. If they are not in place before the project starts, valuable project resources of time and effort will be spent on project infrastructure rather than the objectives of the project itself.

Checklist

- [ ] Development method to cover analysis, design and build
- [ ] Change requests (including negotiation of budget or deadline)
- [ ] Test error reporting and resolution
- [ ] Live error reporting and resolution
- [ ] Deliverable sign-off
- [ ] Test harness installation and running
- [ ] Live installation and handover
- [ ] Project reviews (check on target for delivery date, budget, quality, performance, functionality, goals and requirement matching)
- [ ] Documentation standards
- [ ] Naming conventions for documents, data, program items
- [ ] Configuration from development through testing areas to live environment
- [ ] Issue resolution

Definitions/techniques

None.

Next steps

It is not sufficient to have the above procedures available. Individuals rarely follow procedures written in a project handbook somewhere. The answer is to implement a regimen around the procedures:

- train project staff to use the procedures
- make following the procedures an item in each individual's personal objectives
- make team members responsible for checking compliance with procedures at key points in the project lifecycle
- take ownership of certain critical logs (e.g. issue log, change-request log) to ensure that they are being used.

Naturally, the above procedures can be developed using the checklists throughout this book.

1.6 Determining the big three – targets, timescales and budgets

Type: To do

Checklist description

In the popular IT press, large-scale projects are often reported as over time and over budget – but is it the project or the planning of the project that went wrong? Quite often it is assumed to be the former not the latter. Often the latter is subject to a fixed, pre-project delivery date. One view is that planning should not be constrained by a delivery date – fitting of work to a date is called scheduling.

As with most projects, there is normally some interaction between the plan and the target date. A fair amount of 'horse trading' can be expected as the first-cut plan exceeds the target date and hence alternative configurations of delivery schedule, resources etc. are applied to the plan to bring it in on schedule.

The important rule is to prepare the first-cut plan without reference to the target date. Then the haggling can begin! This checklist can be used to derive the first-cut plan.

Checklist

1   Get an overall estimate for the work involved including timescales:
    - include costs for recruiting extra staff
    - nclude training costs
    - include overhead time costs for meetings, planning, analysis, problem solving and trial-and-error prototyping
    - include an overhead for average productive time (no one is productive full-time – thinking time, socializing, sick leave)
    - ensure the plan includes sufficient time to test, fix and retest.

2   Factor some/all of the estimates for uncertainty:
    - new technology and techniques being deployed
    - experience of staff
    - areas where under-/overestimating has occurred in the past
    - expectation of using contract staff
    - areas where requirements are vague or likely to change
    - see the post-implementation review of previous projects for any other causes of failure
    - add an additional factor for fixing 'unknown bugs' where the system is complex (high number of modules or interfaces). Large, complex systems are more liable to exhibit 'chaotic' behaviour when all its elements are combined.

3   Review plan:
    - check that the delivery of components:
        - is sensible from a testing perspective (e.g. data reporting functionality follows data-creation functionality not the other way round)
        - is business-value led (i.e. high business-value components come first)

- set milestones using:
  - natural breakpoints
  - important deliverables
  - few not many (between 10 and 20) and regularly spaced
  - get a 'quick win' in early
- set activities required to achieve each milestone.

4   Determine team members:
  - set skills and individuals against activities
  - set out reporting lines.

5   Based on the plan, determine the budget which identifies:
  - fixed, known costs
  - hard/soft estimates depending on whether the information used in estimating was reliable, fixed and complete
  - budgets with floors and ceilings for worst/best case scenarios.

Definitions/techniques

None.

Next steps

The plan, at best, is a statement of intent. Whilst plans do try to predict the future, it is not an exact science. The budget is a natural consequence of the plan (as shown above) and, since it is based on uncertain information, is also subject to future changes.

Both, however, should show where information is not fixed and hence give managers an idea where change is expected. What should be avoided is an attempt by managers to remove some of the uncertainties from the plan and budget in order to fit a given timescale or budget. Uncertainty exists, whether they are shown in the plan or budget or not. Hidden uncertainties, like submerged icebergs, can sink a project when they are encountered.

See also checklists 1.4 'How to do a simple risk assessment' and 1.8 'How long is a piece of software?'.

Finally, it's all too easy to cut the budget or timescale based on a target implementation date rather than on the expected economic life of the system. Rather, there should be an endeavour to view the budget or timescale for quality software on a long-term, system-life basis rather than on the length of the development project (short term). It's important to bear this in mind when the haggling starts.

1.7   Nine tell-tale signs of a project nightmare

Type: Analysis

Checklist description

Projects are not 'the stuff that dreams are made of'. Rather, some projects are absolute nightmares. Quite often, signs that the project is going to be a nightmare can be detected early on. The source of these signals is generally the board, the project sponsor or the person who is recruiting you or your company to conduct the project.

Although this checklist is slightly tongue-in-cheek, I have genuinely heard all of these phrases in real project kick-off meetings (and wished I'd said the retort in only some of them!).

You can use this checklist to:

- play 'kick-off meeting' bingo – get more than 5 and you win (or lose depending on your point of view)
- decide whether to take the project
- argue it out there and then (some suggested retorts are provided)
- note the issues raised for an 'off-line' discussion of project risk – whether it can be managed and whether it's worth the risk.

Checklist

1   'We have an aggressive timescale.'

Some retorts:
(a)   'How quickly do you want me to get it wrong?'
(b)   'Great – the budget must be fantastic – and I get to spend it all!'
(c)   'I can see we're talking quantity not quality here.'

2   'You will have the resources you want when they become available.'

A retort:
(a)   'That's okay, you'll get the deliverable you want when it becomes available.'

3   'The steering group/board hasn't got the time to discuss this so assume "yes" for now.'

Some retorts:
(a)   'So time and materials are okay on this project?'
(b)   'Let's not ask the steering group/board. What do they know anyway?'
(c)   'Tell you what, let's assume 'no' – it's far more interesting and less of a political risk.'

4   'We can't afford to disrupt the business.'

A retort:
'Then we can't afford to do the project. The risks already outweigh the benefits.'

5   'There are some business/people issues to sort out but don't worry that's not your problem.'

Some retorts:
(a)   'What are they?' (Bound to confuse as they don't expect you to want to be involved.)

(b) 'Whose problem is it?' (ditto)

(c) Sarcastically – 'Oh sure.'

6 'Because of the fast turnaround we need on this one, just set up a crack team of programmers to push it through.'

Some retorts:

(a) 'Just think of all that maintenance and bug fixing – jobs for life.'

(b) 'Great – I get to do some coding myself then.'

7 'My staff are too busy so I will represent them on the requirements study.'

Some retorts:

(a) 'They'll be delighted. Can you train them in the system too?'

(b) 'I bet my guys know what you want anyway. Let's just let them code it.'

(c) 'You mean your department doesn't need you to manage it?'

8 'Here's the deadline now start planning the project to deliver to it.'

Some retorts:

(a) 'I won't need the deadline. Once I start this project, they won't cancel it.'

(b) 'There goes the testing phase (again)!'

9 'The MD has agreed it so I don't want a cost/benefit analysis. It's a done deal.'

Some retorts:

(a) 'That will give me something to tell the auditors when they start asking awkward questions.'

(b) 'That's all right. I couldn't see there were going to be any benefits anyway.'

(c) 'Don't you just love IT. Every project gets its own blank cheque!'

Definitions/techniques

None.

Next steps

On a more serious note, if any of the above phrases do appear in project inception meetings, you need to:

- be non-committal about the project until you have investigated further
- investigate further, specifically:
  - How big is the risk? (See checklist 1.4 'How to do a simple risk assessment')
  - Is the project feasible or impossible with the constraints imposed?
  - What could be changed about the constraints that makes the project feasible?
  - Is the project worth the risk to the business?
  - Have you worked successfully under these conditions before (and are you happy to do so again)?
- report back as to whether you are or are not committed to delivering the project under these conditions and use your analysis to negotiate to a better position (even if this is 'no project').

Ultimately, the project will be **your** project and **you** must decide whether you want to work in a nightmare scenario or not. It will be easier to sort this out upfront rather than in mid-flight.

1.8 How long is a piece of software?

Type: To do

Checklist description

There are four basic types of method for estimating a project:

1   Expert – 'guesstimation'.

2   Analogy – that project took so long, this is like it so it will take a similar time.

3   Decomposition – break down projects into smaller chunks and estimate them based on low level industry experience.

4   Equation – mathematical model of software projects.

What makes it difficult to measure?

- Software is intangible.
- Each piece of software is built afresh using different techniques and languages by people of different ability and knowledge of the business the application is trying to support.
- Company culture, development team makeup and culture, ergonomic factors (e.g. office layout, space, heat, lighting) can all have an effect.
- Developers change employers rapidly hence difficult to build a reliable pattern of through-put.
- Project specifications are subject to a high degree of change so what was estimated isn't what you are building.
- People are typically overoptimistic and wanting-to-please, have a 'rosy' view of previous development and often only know part of what went into the previous system – hence they are bad sources of estimates.

Why bother?

- It is a requirement to work out development timescales (or, if charging, how much).
- Staffing levels need to be set.
- In short, planning is essential.

Below is a list of the main methods that can be used to support an estimating exercise.

Checklist

Cocomo method (Constructive Cost Model)
Description
   Based on measurement of number of lines of source code, the capability of staff, the complexity of the project and other factors. Uses historic values to give a man-year-effort estimate of old projects based on that value.
Problems
   How do you know how many lines of code?
   Historic systems often written using old languages and technology – do they equate?
How to
   Dr B. Boehm analysed projects to give two equations:

EFFORT $= A^*(KDSI)^{**}B$
DURATION $= C^*(EFFORT)^{**}D$
where
KDSI $=$ thousands of lines of delivered source instructions.

A, B, C, D depend on the type of development:

Development type	A	B	C	D
Organic	3.2	1.05	2.5	.38
Semi-detached	3.0	1.12	2.5	.35
Embedded	2.8	1.2	2.5	.32

Organic – home-grown, standalone system.
Semi-detached – system with some interface to other systems.
Embedded – highly interfaced system which has to work reliably with other systems/hardware.
The resulting calculation could then be weighted by cost-driving factors:

- required reliability
- system complexity
- required reusability
- staff skill
- system environment
- use of development tools or methods.

For example, a normal programmer might be given a multiplier of 1 (no effect) but a junior programmer might be given a multiplier of 1.5. Each different cost driver would have a multiplier value which are all multiplied together.

Function-Point Analysis – formal
Description
Widely used technique (so why do we get it wrong so often?) based on work at IBM. Uses five aspects of software application: inputs, outputs, user queries, data files updated and interfaces. These remain fairly static early on in the development cycle and hence not subject to vagaries of programming language etc.
Problems
There is a subjective element to the generation of function points. Is this an interface or just the production of a file? Is this simple or medium or complex? Does complexity depend on which environment or language you intend to use? Also translating function points to man-days effort (without regard for the skill of the developer) is highly subjective.
How to
Produce a matrix of counts of the following elements split by simple, medium, complex:

- external input type – number of input and update transactions
- external output type – number of reports
- logical internal file type – number of files and/or tables used
- external interface file type – number of feeder files to/from another system
- external enquiry type – number of read-only displays to the user.

Apply the weightings for each simple, medium, complex count to give it a 'raw' function point score.

Function elements	Simple	Medium	Complex
External input type	3	4	6
External output type	4	5	7
Logical internal file type	7	10	15
External interface type	5	7	10
External enquiry type	3	4	6

There are modifiers of complexity for each of the above elements:

1 Function is performed over a telecommunications network.
2 Data or processing is distributed (e.g. client server).
3 Requirements for throughput or response time are demanding.
4 Application will run on an already busy machine.
5 System will be used daily.
6 On-line data entry and validation is a key part of the system.
7 There are a large volume of transactions.
8 On-line functions have to be carefully mapped to user activity.
9 System components are to be reused.
10 System is complex to install.
11 System will be implemented on a number of sites.
12 System will be difficult to maintain.

For each element/adjustment factor, the following scores should be totalled:

0 – not applicable/significant
1 – insignificant influence
2 – moderate influence
3 – average influence
4 – significant influence
5 – strong influence

It is now possible to calculate the function point for each element:

function point = 'raw' function point * ((adjustment total)/100)

The function points can then be used as a measure of how many man-days effort are required to produce the function, e.g. five function points = one man-day. The best way to derive this value is to produce a function-point analysis on an already completed set of functions where the actual effort is already known.

Function-Point Analysis – some refinements
Description
   Function point analysis can be applied in many areas of a development project. Quite often estimates are required in advance of a formal design so the above method cannot be used. Below are several other areas where function points could be allocated as part of an estimation exercise.
Problems
   As with formal function-point analysis, allocating points and then translating points to man-days is highly subjective. Building in a estimate–build–revise feedback loop to revise the function point to man-days equation can be a powerful remedy to this 'subjective' drawback.

How to

For estimating the requirements gathering process, apply function points based on:

- how many business processes does it involve?
- how many users?
- how many user departments?
- how complex is each business process (number of interactions, tasks etc.)?

For estimating the complexity of a function – apply function points based on the number of:

- business rules
- decision points
- variables
- outputs
- inputs
- stored data items – file, record and field
- screens and reports.

For estimating the size of a system for testing purposes, apply function points based on:

- number of business rules
- number of decision points
- number of screens
- number of fields per screen
- number of reports
- number of fields per report
- complexity rating of screens and reports
- amount of data stored and retrieval method
- complexity of algorithms
- complexity of calculations.

Definitions/techniques

None.

Next steps

Peter Drucker once asserted, 'You can't manage what you can't measure.' Estimation using the above techniques will give some form of measurement. It now has to be managed.

Obviously the raw estimate(s) provided from above may need to be factored further for:

- contingency (i.e. no one is 100 per cent efficient 100 per cent of the time – unproductive time needs to be factored in)
- risk – not everything is known upfront
- individual experience and productivity (e.g. senior developers are expected to produce quality code faster than junior developers).

For more information on applying estimates see checklist 1.6 'Determining the big three – targets, timescales and budgets'.

1.9   How should I staff a project?

Type: Analysis

Checklist description

Computers don't produce computer systems, people do. When involved in projects, people are the most important factor for success. Yet still many projects are set up with the people available rather than the people who are needed. People are seen as the most adaptable attribute in a project and therefore 'anything goes'. However, projects run and staffed by 'square pegs in round holes' will invariably overrun time and cost constraints and produce a lower quality product.

Obviously this is a large and complex subject. This checklist is only a 'starter for ten' set of guidelines on staffing a project.

Checklist

1   Use your best people:

There is a wide productivity gap between the best IT performers and the average or below average IT performers. It has been asserted that the top 20 per cent produce 50 per cent of the finished system and the bottom 50 per cent produce only 20 per cent. If your project is highly constrained by time, cost and quality – be prepared to pay for the best. So what if they're double the cost, they will actually do the job you want.

2   Match jobs to people's skills and motivation:

(a)   Realize that managers don't motivate people. People can only motivate themselves.

(b)   Rather than promote people to the level of their own incompetence, allow people to progress into the area they wish to specialize in.

(c)   This will allow people to maintain high levels of motivation rather than being swapped to a job they don't actually want and in which they struggle. The final demotivational blow will come when they realize they have been parked with no room to manoeuvre back to their old position without loss of standing in the organization.

(d)   Note that it is the combination of skill and motivation that is important. Many people become disaffected with a company because they have been stuck maintaining a system in which they are the only expert.

3   Allow people to grow:

(a)   Once people satisfy their basic remuneration wants, they seek to self-actualize to realize their full potential.

(b)   This could mean:

(i)   develop in a specialist area
(ii)   develop in a broad area
(iii)   be the architect/designer/builder of something successful
(iv)   take time off for extra-curricular activities.

(c)   As people get more and more comfortable in their current area, they need opportunities to self-actualize and, if you don't provide them, they will take steps to find them elsewhere. Hence a whole range of rewards needs to be available which people may select according to what is appropriate to them:

    (i)   training courses (e.g. specialist IT courses)
    (ii)   funding for outside training (e.g. management diplomas/degrees)
    (iii) ability to take paid/unpaid sabbaticals
    (iv) full-time to part-time options (and reversal)
    (v)   funding for research projects (work related or otherwise).

(d)   These types of options can be awarded on a performance-related points system.

(e)   As stated earlier, accept that you cannot motivate people, people motivate themselves. What you have to do is create a climate of opportunity.

(f)   The biggest motivation 'win–win' is where a person's goals overlap with the organization's goals. Surprisingly, a large number of individuals want to be associated with success – a successful, well-run project and implementation is extremely attractive.

4   Build a balanced team:

(a)   Since most IT projects require a mix of activities, a team needs to be a balanced set of skills especially if a large proportion of them are specialists in their field:

    (i)   customer/user negotiation
    (ii)   generation of user requirements
    (iii) systems design
    (iv) system build
    (v)   testing
    (vi) documentation
    (vii) training
    (viii) technical infrastructure build, implementation and maintenance.

(b)   Also a team needs to be balanced in terms of personality and temperament in order to promote team working:

    (i)   co-operation
    (ii)   sharing of problems
    (iii) generation of solutions
    (iv) sharing of knowledge.

Often the skills mix is attended to without regard to the personality mix. However, unbalanced teams will become less and less productive as politics and 'turf wars' take over leading to increased isolationism on behalf of the team members.

5   Manage the team mix:

(a)   It is extremely difficult to know at the moment of team creation whether the mix is correct and will be successful – so it needs to be monitored.

(b)   Leaving someone on the team who doesn't fit is eventually counterproductive. Other team members will:

    (i)   resent that no action has been taken
    (ii)   resent that they have to 'cover'.

(c)   Note that some individuals may have a direct contribution to team deliverables and some individuals' contributions may be indirect (e.g. a quality checker, a morale booster etc.). Be careful of 'moving on' someone if the team perceives that person is vital to the effort even if their direct contribution seems low.

(d) Changing the constituents of a team needs careful and sensitive planning, including:
- (i) ensuring confidentiality
- (ii) acknowledge your own responsibility in the formation of the team and its continued operation
- (iii) giving the person 'due process':
    - fairness and impartiality
    - listening without having made a final decision
    - comprehensive fact finding and checking – separating fact from opinion
    - taking time to 'get it right'
    - earnestly wanting the best for the other person
    - being prepared to balance the good of the person with the good of the team
- (iv) work hard to find a new role in another area or project that is a better guarantee of success (i.e. no pushing the person out to be someone else's problem)
- (v) finding the right niche for this person may mean going beyond the boundaries of the current organization. If this is the case, it should be faced honestly and with integrity. Provided that you aim at finding what's best for the person rather than what's best for the company, it can be promoted as a positive development rather than a negative one.

Definitions/techniques

None.

Next steps

Selecting individuals with the right skills for the project is only part of the team-building process. There are a number of other areas that need to be addressed. For example:

- team structure – roles and responsibilities
- recognition and reward mechanisms
- performance monitoring and evaluation
- objective setting
- training
- team building and team culture.

Obviously, the treatment in this book is merely scratching the surface. If more detail is required, including more formal methods for selecting team members, there are plenty of books available in the marketplace.

Having team members is only part of the project set-up process, procedures need to be put in place that show the team how it is meant to interact with one another – see checklist 1.5 'Twelve project procedures to have in place before you start'.

1.10   Project trade-offs – how to tease them out upfront

Type: To do

Checklist description

Almost all IT projects have an associated set of elements that have to be managed. Typically, there are a set of features to deliver, a target date and a set of resources. However, it is well known that these elements are at odds with each other: it may not be possible to deliver all of the features by the target date. Hence there is a trade-off: move the target date or drop some of the features.

However, at the early stages of a project, it may appear that all the features can be delivered within the timescale using the given resources. It is only as a project progresses that some of the 'guesstimates' begin to unravel. This is not surprising since no one knows the future and a great many things can affect a project adversely including project complexity, staff turnover, business strategy etc.

Hence it is important to specify how those trade-offs will be managed at the start of the project. This gives the project manager and the project sponsor a framework for future decision making on the project when the unexpected arrives.

This checklist can be used to produce a project trade-off matrix.

Checklist

1   Create a matrix as follows:

	Optimize	Limit	Allow flexibility
Resources			
Target date			
Features/quality			

2   The conditional settings have the following effects:
  (a) Optimize – means to seek the best in this area; use it to determine the key success criteria for the project.
  (b) Limit – means to place some thresholds so that the project works within expected boundaries.
  (c) Allow flexibility – means that this element can vary in order to allow the other elements to meet their conditional settings.

3   Discuss with the project sponsor, the options available as follows:
  (a) To optimize:
    (i)   resources means to seek the minimum amount of people possible (i.e. minimum cost strategy)
    (ii)   target date means to ship as early as possible (i.e. time critical)
    (iii) features is to seek maximum benefit – ship as many features as possible.

(b) To limit:
   (i)   resources is to place a maximum on the number of people involved
   (ii)   target date is to time-box the project (it cannot go beyond this date)
   (iii) features or quality is to set a base level of functionality that must be met
(c) To remain flexible over:
   (i)   resources is to adopt a time plus materials project costing basis (beware of the mythical man month!) in order to achieve required functionality or meet the target date
   (ii)   target date is to allow this to slip in order to achieve the functionality or keep costs and resources at a minimum
   (iii) features is to allow features not to be delivered to meet the target date or prevent extra spend in producing them.

4   With the project sponsor, place a tick in each of the three rows and columns such that each row has only one tick in it and each column has only one tick in it. Any other combination allowed (e.g. two ticks in one column and none in another etc.) is a serious project risk and could potentially jeopardize the successful completion of the project.

5   Use this matrix for decision making. It should be incorporated in the Project Charter/Risk Management document.

Definitions/techniques

Mythical Man Month – from Peter Drucker's book. The principle is essentially that people and time are not directly interchangeable as some project management techniques might imply. If you have a hundred man-days' work ahead, adding one hundred people to the project does not mean that it can be done in a day. In fact, the principle asserts that adding people to a 'late' project can make it later. This observation is based on the fact that new people have learning curves which slow the project down. These people absorb time from the current project workers/ managers making the existing staff less productive.

Next steps

Note that the key ingredient in this process is understanding and agreeing, not necessarily documenting. Some people have an obsession with documents (Neville Chamberlain for one!). Just because something is on paper does not mean it is understood or agreed.

Similarly, the project sponsor needs to be the pig in the bacon and eggs breakfast project scenario: the chicken was involved in the project but the pig was definitely committed.

1.11   What sort of project lifecycle should I adopt?

Type: Analysis

Checklist description

All projects have a lifecycle. Projects by definition have a beginning, middle and end, or birth, life and death. However, what happens between birth and death can vary enormously. The life of a project can be structured, or chaotic, or somewhere in between.

Various methods (or methodologies) for systems development have been proposed – but how do you pick between them?

This checklist will give a brief outline of some of the common development approaches and what their relative merits and demerits are.

Checklist

Waterfall development

Waterfall approach – a systems development method (like SSADM) where the outputs of one phase of analysis form the inputs of the next phase, the final output being the completed system.

Advantages:

- easily understood
- gives clear sign-off points on agreed deliverables
- can use a variety of techniques to produce the deliverable – whichever seem most appropriate to the task in hand
- fairly 'tried and tested' method for large-scale developments.

Disadvantages:

- can be slow since work on the next phase of development is dependent on the output of the previous phase
- its slowness means that the organization's requirements have changed significantly from project inception to project implementation – thus making the new system potentially redundant on the day of its launch
- tends to limit end-user input which leads to a lack of ownership of the new system   this can cause serious implementation issues as individuals resist the change because it is being 'forced' on them without their 'consent'
- limited end-user involvement also places the burden of how the system supports the business process in the hands of developers. The developers will rarely understand the business problems that the software is trying to solve and may design the system such that it is impracticable in the real world
- mistakes early in the project have a cascading effect of errors later in the project
- depends on good documentation skills.

RAD, prototyping, iterative development

This method involves iterating between requirements gathering and systems development until a usable system is produced.

Advantages:

It can be used when:

- a 'quick and dirty' solution is acceptable
- businesses are happy to work around 'bugs'
- data quality is not a key issue
- the system is a throwaway
- the system is standalone (i.e. no interfaces)
- the system is primarily screen based to present, capture, store data rather than an extensive back-end batch process (which can't easily be demonstrated to a user for comment)
- it's easy to test
- a working version of the system can be produced within months at a quality that will be acceptable to the business in the first instance
- the system is not mission critical
- developer expectations match their abilities and the task in hand
- business expectations match the quality they are likely to encounter in a prototyping scenario.

Disadvantages:

It should not be used when:

- the delivery of the system is subject to fixed-price, fixed-quality contract
- the system to be delivered is an enhancement of an existing system and where you are constrained by its design
- the customer expects every requirement to be present (irrespective of cost benefit or time available) – time-boxing inevitably means that some requirements are thrown out as irrelevant or impossible
- complex cases are required to test the system
- documentation will be required to maintain the system
- you wish to hide the development process for commercial or political reasons (e.g. you don't want to show how cheap it is to produce certain features, your programmers code in the nude etc.)
- business users won't commit to serious tranches of their time
- easy to have 'scope-creep' – keep to the original objectives for the time-box and get management to insist on another time-box for other functions
- susceptible to hidden agendas or swamping by management of end-users' input
- developers may not be happy with the level of customer contact – they may feel intimidated and exposed to scrutiny
- developer/end-user may get isolated from their natural habitat (a) in the workplace and (b) socially (especially if working away from home)
- beware of too many decisions being taken out of the end-user's/developer's joint working hands. This will cause an ownership/blame issue later
- unsuitable for inexperienced or fractious development team.

Object Orientation (OO)

Object orientation attempts to simplify the development process by trying to mimic the real world more closely. Hence, within an OO system, real-world objects should exist as system objects (e.g. customer, car, purchase order). The OO system then attempts to maintain the natural relationships between these objects (e.g. customer submits purchase order to buy car). By mimicking the real world so closely, OO claims that maintenance is lower (the behaviour of real-world objects is fairly fixed) and reuse is higher (a customer object can be used by more than one application).

Advantages:

- data hiding – objects can be complex underneath but only show 'real-world' data for other objects to use
- changes limited to a few places – all the customer processing is within the customer object
- easily understood in the first instance – most people recognize the real-world objects and understand their behaviour.

Disadvantages:

- databases still not handling objects, i.e. very few programming environments let you move seemlessly from Object-Orientated Design (OOD) to an object-orientated system. Object orientation differs from RDBMS since in RDBMS links are established by looking up keys in each table. In OO, links are explicit connections between instances, i.e. a foreign key would be replaced with a link
- can get too many small objects which are hard to keep track of and use
- depends heavily on good cataloguing and library use by developers (not invented here syndrome)
- difficult to plan for reuse unless you can envisage the reuse
- difficult to use where there is not much data storage – e.g. primarily scientific calculations = few objects plus complex methods.

Definitions/techniques

Time-boxing – fixing the amount of time spent on a particular phase in a project. This has a tendency to clarify the scope of the work in hand and cut out anything which is superfluous to 'must-have' functionality.

Scope-creep – where additional requirements keep being added into the project without any control or reference to the project's original objectives.

'Not Invented Here' (NIH) syndrome – a 'trust' issue whereby developers would rather use their own code than borrow someone else's.

Next steps

It is important not to fool yourself (or others) over the analysis of the above issues. Business managers like the idea of 'rapid applications' because it sounds like they get something for (almost) nothing. However, like lunches, there's no such thing as a free application. Computer systems are inherently complex and the complexity rises with the number and quality of functions to be delivered.

Don't try to be rapid, try to be right. The use of prototyping should be seen as an attempt to get closer to what the business wants – not necessarily to cut timescales. Shorter timescales only occur when the final system is so close to what the business wants. Then there is no need for a maintenance cycle to upgrade a three-year-old waterfall-approach development to what the business requires now.

If, honestly, the business would rather have a far from perfect system soon than a near-perfect system sometime and if you have sufficient confidence in the team (business practitioners, analysts, developers) to deliver then prototyping may be worth trying.

Note, if you are rolling out the method across more than one project, check that you have not developed a 'one size fits all' mentality. There is nothing wrong with having several different methods provided individuals have been trained to know when and how to use each one. Some different types of project requiring different methods might be:

- full-scale development based on requirements
- fast-path development and/or prototyping
- change control and maintenance
- package evaluation, acquisition, implementation
- infrastructure work (data warehouse, corporate database, ERP/CRM)
- different programming paradigms (green screen, client server, Internet).

See also checklist 5.2 'How do you make a methodology?'.

1.12   Make or buy – deciding the package or bespoke development question

Type: Analysis

Checklist description

There are four basic options to systems development:

1   Make it yourself – internal bespoke.

2   Get someone to make it for you – external bespoke.

3   Buy a package – package only.

4   Buy a package and have it altered to suit – tailored package.

Each option has its own advantages/disadvantages. Naturally, it is possible to make every advantage of a particular option the disadvantage of another. However, this has not been done since more ground can be covered in a shorter space if this logical connection is taken for granted.

Each option should be considered for its relative merits/demerits in your situation.

Checklist

Internal bespoke (make)
Advantages:

- Project workers are directly answerable on simple contractual terms – hire and fire. The company can decide who works on what project – a totally controllable resource. This is a large factor in the reduction of risk.
- The development can change as the business changes although it is not instantaneous.
- Support is more readily available and more immediate. Knowledge is in-house and has a background in the company context and culture.
- An internal team has more commitment to develop good relationships after the 'sale' since they have to live with the system and its users afterwards. They only have one client to please.
- There is a good supply of additional skills and resources depending on market conditions.
- The quality of internal work undertaken is controllable by the company. Managers can insist on quality controls and inspections at every stage of the build process. The quality of external work is unknown and must be verified by competent in-house personnel, otherwise low quality is hidden and not discovered until it is too late.
- It enables the company to maintain core skills and competence in-house. IT strategy must be owned and directed in-house. If the company doesn't have an internal resource able to do this, suppliers can end up calling the shots.
- Business knowledge is retained in-house.

Disadvantages:

- The team may not have the right skill-set especially in terms of user training, user documentation etc.

- The development may become dependent on a few individuals which may jeopardize the project if they leave.
- It is a lengthy process involving the IT department and senior management making the cost of such a system high.
- Internal development necessitates investing money in non-core activities, i.e. producing computer systems.
- The development may be subject to a higher level of changes (hence a lengthier, more costly development) to the original specification since the business managers feel less constrained about new requests and change-control procedures are more easily by-passed.
- Certain skills are only required intermittently. It makes sense only to buy these in when needed.
- The team can get overcommitted to one particular computer architecture or method, ignoring good business solutions because they 'don't fit'.
- The team can get reluctant to purchase packages, preferring to develop everything in-house as part of protection or empire building.
- An in-house resource is more apt to be involved in company politics since it is a resource to be controlled.

Package only (buy)

Advantages:

- Shorter timescales than other new systems methods although this is not necessarily immediate due to availability, conversion and training constraints. This can lead to early payback compared to the 'make' process.
- Although the price includes an element of the supplier's profit, the unit cost of the software is cheaper since it has been developed once and sold several times.
- It is possible to see the system and try it out before purchase.
- Usually it is expected that quality is higher since the package is likely to be tried and tested – but this is not always the case. However, suppliers normally can refer to reference sites where the package is currently in use.
- There is a body of existing users whose experience can be called upon. Also, due to their broad base of experience, the product can be developed to be a more rounded, maturer product.
- Usually, they are comparatively cheap and there are many suppliers to choose from (which gives greater bargaining power) especially if a commodity package is required (payroll, accounting, software tool etc.).This is not so true if the required system is strategic or close to the heart of the business where there is potential competitive advantage.
- All the headaches of software development problems are effectively transferred from in-house to external suppliers – they are one less thing to be concerned about.
- User documentation and training courses already exist and do not have to be set up from scratch.

Disadvantages:

- The company needs to have expert buyers and managers of external suppliers. Also, there is a need for an excellent method for capturing and filtering requirements as well as a method for shortlisting potential packages.
- The company does not have direct access to the actual developers and managers. The

company is really forced to deal with the supplier's protective skin – the help desk. Over a distance, the lines of communication may become strained or crossed.

- What is important to the supplier may be different to the importance of the company. Response to problems may be adversely prioritized by the supplier and problems requiring an instant response may not be forthcoming.
- Maintenance charges can be high at around 20 per cent of the original purchase price per annum. Also, sundry fixes/changes, use of help desk etc. may be charged at premium rates.
- The company must watch suppliers' competitors to see if the deal is still good.
- The speed of changes and improvements will not be dictated solely by the company but by the marketplace (i.e. other customers requesting the same improvement). The company is only one of several customers and may be prioritized in terms of its relative importance to the supplier's other customers. Also some changes may remove or change key or much-loved features. This may lead to the company being left in a development cul-de-sac (i.e. unwilling to upgrade and unwilling to forego certain features).
- The package may match business requirements by a fair degree but some key features are omitted. This may mean either business re-engineering to work round or lose certain business activities or pay for modifications (see next section on a modified package).
- The company may end up paying for features it does not need or want.
- The company may find features that it requests for competitive advantage (e.g. support for a new market niche) being offered as a standard feature to all the supplier's customers – the company's competitors.
- It is more difficult to convert from an internal system to an external system since detailed knowledge is required of both systems.
- The company may be forced to upgrade. This may also involve a hardware change if a support agreement between package and hardware supplier lapses.
- The company may not find a supplier with an integrated suite of applications that covers the business functions it wishes to automate. Some development will be required to build the right interfaces between them. This also leads to having to deal with several suppliers.
- There may be some alienation among internal IT development staff – the 'Not Invented Here' (NIH) syndome. IT personnel may resent the adoption of a package that they wished to write and may feel they could have done a better job at a cheaper price.

Modified package (buy and make)

Advantages:

- The company gets the system it wants. It can specify changes and the look and feel of the system as well as its sequence of operations, additional data and validations.
- The source code may be available for purchase which may mean that some of the package disadvantages are circumvented (see Package only section).
- It may be possible to buy the source code of the package and separately tender out required modifications (or bring them in-house) to reduce costs, decrease dependence on the supplier or utilize some other resource.

Disadvantages:

- Expensive in terms of time to implement and costs. It is sometimes much more difficult to upgrade when a new, improved version comes out because the modifications have to be reapplied.

- The required changes may be squeezed into the package design so that:
  - further product upgrades are not possible
  - further modifications are more difficult and hence more costly
  - performance of the system is seriously degraded.
- The delivery timescale may be as long as starting from scratch.
- The company is still involved in activities associated with producing computer systems: requirements analysis, systems analysis etc. However, under package selection, it is probably paying for expensive specialist contractors as well as the involvement of internal senior management.
- The supplier may withdraw support from the company's implementation since it is too costly for them to support too many variants.

Definitions/techniques

None.

Next steps

Depending on the nature of the system, it should be possible to rank some of the above pros and cons to indicate what solution might be applicable.

If a package or hybrid package/bespoke solution is chosen as the preferred approach, some careful attention to the package-selection process should be made. See checklist 1.13 'Some do's and don'ts of package selection'.

1.13 Some do's and don'ts of package selection

Type: Analysis

Checklist description

Software package selection is a process in its own right. Naturally, some of the checklists on identifying business needs and software requirements still need to be conducted regardless of whether a package or bespoke solution is adopted.

The following checklist is a set of recommendations to put in place for a package-selection project.

Checklist

Some do's

- Be careful not to select on price over usability, functionality, vendor-maturity and vendor market stability.
- Allow time to go through the process.
- Get the right people involved in the evaluation.
- Ensure business benefit is paramount and measure all slippage and additional costs against the benefit. It's better to pull out costing a small amount than a large amount.
  - Does the sequence of transactions match our business process? How much change to, retraining/rethinking of, our business processes is required?
  - How much data conversion is required? Is it included in the price?
  - Is our technical architecture compatible? How much change or upgrade is required? Will this involve a serious departure from our current skills base? How much of a dependency is there on key staff and is this a risk?
  - What is the upgrade path?
- Be cautious over new releases.
  - Realize that each new package or version of the package may fix old bugs but will come with new bugs.
  - Ensure that all releases of the product are fully tested, i.e. existing functionality still works.
  - Assess the impact and cost of upgrades and whether business benefits will accrue from making the change.
- Review the options for unwanted features in a product.
  - Can it be switched off?
  - Can costs be reduced if this function is removed or not provided?
  - Does the system capture all the data you require? Some? Most? All? All and then some? Is there 'over-the-top' data mandatory in the package and what is your additional cost of collecting it?

Some don'ts

- Avoid supervising the vendor – they need to be managed to come up with your solution.
- Avoid protecting the board from the vendor – needs board-level involvement.
- Have a cast-iron specification or contract that doesn't allow for change.

- Have a licence that means increases in user base, machines and subsidiary companies will cost a fortune to add to the licence.
- Suppress all criticism of the supplier or their product. Invite criticism and handle it. Verify its truth or otherwise and take action.
- Skimp on testing assuming it has been done by the supplier. Test it yourself for what you want it to do including its interfaces to your other systems.

Definitions/techniques

None.

Next steps

Regardless of whether systems are packages or home-grown, they still have to be implemented. See Chapter 8 'System implementation checklists' for more information on package installation.

2
Project control checklists

2.1 Five things to be checked throughout the project lifecycle

Type: Analysis

Checklist description

Now the project is underway with a project plan, people following the prescribed project method, and deliverables in production, what should a project manager be doing as part of the process?

This checklist in intended to help build mechanisms that kick in at relevant stages of the project to monitor the following.

Checklist

1   Project phases and milestones:
    (a)   Apply 'stop' criteria for each project phase. Determine when the phase deliverables are 'good enough'. Otherwise too much time may be spent adding low value 'polish'.
    (b)   Apply 'early warning' criteria and project checkpoints to prevent overrun on budget or timescale (see checklist 2.2 'Spotting a project runaway before it happens').

2   Quality:
    (a)   Quality cannot be added to a product at the end. It has to be built in from the start.
    (b)   Quality can be built in by the prevention of defects.
    (c)   To prevent defects, a project manager should ensure the following exist:
        (i)   a set of build procedures/processes that are understood by the entire project team (see checklist 5.1 'What should be in a methodology?')
        (ii) build standards for every deliverable (whether an internal deliverable or an external deliverable) – see 'Standards' below
        (iii) testing for every deliverable – see 'Testing' below
        (iv) a quality feedback loop to enhance the procedures and standards.

3   Standards:
    (a)   Module layout standards (e.g. header, global data area, local data area, i/o handover area etc.).
    (b)   Screen and report layout standards.
    (c)   Naming conventions:
        (i)   file naming conventions and directory structure standards
        (ii) naming guidelines could include:
            ●   length of names
            ●   how compound names are formed – which is the prefix/suffix?
            ●   use of separators – dashes, slashes, underscores
            ●   standard abbreviations
            ●   keep an eye on alpha sorting for grouping things in directory listings etc.
            ●   object typing within the name.

4   Testing:
    (a)   Start testing early – don't leave to final part of project.
    (b)   Carry out testing at each project stage.

(c) Test for each deliverable for:
   (i) verification – building the right product:
      * does this meet our project goal?
      * is it the sort of deliverable expected?
      * has it got the 'ring of truth'?
   (ii) validation – building the product right:
      * internally consistent
      * to standards
      * has the 'ring of quality'
      * meets satisfaction and performance criteria.

5 Configuration management:
(a) As a project continues, a large number of items are produced:
   (i) requirements specifications
   (ii) design specifications
   (iii) screen layout
   (iv) report layout
   (v) database schema
   (vi) programs
   (vii) test scripts.

(b) Project knowledge also grows. Refinements to requirements can be found even in the testing phase. These refinements might:
   (i) change the database so that programs need to capture or use the changed data item (e.g. make a screen change)
   (ii) need a business rule to be changed in all programs affected by the rule.

(c) For full project control, it should be possible to determine a consistent set of specifications and programs that can be delivered together.

(d) This requires the project manager to put in place:
   (i) procedures which determine when things are signed off as complete
   (ii) a means for securing signed-off material so that it cannot be changed without authorization
   (iii) a procedure for moving previously 'signed-off' material into an area for change.

Definitions/techniques

None.

Next steps

Plans and procedure manuals state intentions but it is not the plan or procedure which makes things happen – it is the project manager.

Project plans typically contain the activity for all team members but not for the project manager. There does also need to be a plan for the project manager which contains regular project checkpoints and milestones to ensure all the above is happening.

Among others, the checklist 2.2 'Spotting a project runaway before it happens' may be helpful.

2.2 Spotting a project runaway before it happens

Type: To do

Checklist description

Unattended projects can just run and run, absorbing resources, money, and time. Often, runaway projects are only detected when a budget limit is exceeded or a deadline is missed. What is needed is an 'early warning' system to detect projects before they become runaways.

To do this, a project manager/sponsor must set their own project checkpoints which co-exist with the project milestones. This checklist will help a manager to use a plan and budget to set these internal checkpoints.

Checklist

1   Determine the milestone(s) to measure. The milestone could be one or more of:
    (a) target date
    (b) budget
    (c) other resource utilization.

2   For the milestone, set a **maximum** tolerance figure as a percentage:
    (a) This figure is what the milestone can realistically overrun by.
    (b) This value should be a maximum. In other words, if it is determined that the project would exceed this maximum, it would be cancelled, no matter what the circumstances.
    (c) Some typical values may be:
        (i)   10 per cent
        (ii) 20 per cent
        (iii) 25 per cent.

3   Set a project checkpoint as the target minus the tolerance:
    (a) For example, if the target is 100 with a tolerance of 25 per cent then the checkpoint is 75.
    (b) If the tolerance is small (e.g. 10 per cent), it may be wise to set the checkpoint to be target minus 2 or 3 times the tolerance.

4   Maintain a regular watch as to when the project exceeds the project checkpoint value.

5   When the project checkpoint is reached, apply the 'runaway test':
    (a) For example, if the tolerance is 25 per cent, ask yourself both these questions:
        (i)   with one-third of the effort spent so far, will the project or deliverable be completed?
        (ii) with two-thirds of the effort spent so far, will the project or deliverable be completed?
    (b) The 'one-third/two-thirds' test will change according to the tolerance value.

6   Assess whether a runaway project is in progress:
    (a) If the answer to both of these is 'no', flag the project as a runaway – it's currently within target but will be way off target by completion.

(b) A discussion is required with the project sponsor(s), manager(s) and the team to either:
    (i) cancel the project
    (ii) give it a serious rethink – its aims and objectives, its function coverage, its quality and its development method.

Definitions/techniques

None.

Next steps

Although it is subjective to estimate how much more work, budget etc. is required, this method can detect a runaway project before the entire budget has been spent.

Do, however, be aware of the subjective. It's all right to say something is 99 per cent complete if it will only take 1 per cent more effort to finish it. It's not all right to say something is 99 per cent complete if it will actually take 300 per cent more effort to complete the final 1 per cent.

This is a powerful damage-limitation technique since it will save the company money. Certainly, money and time have already been spent. But, by adopting this technique, you could be saving up to 50 per cent of the resources that would have been spent in the vain hope of completing the project.

Apart from the subjective estimating issue, the other problem with applying this technique is honesty. It is hard to abandon something once started. There is a psychological barrier to admitting that something is failing. This, in turn, can lead to false optimism, hoping that 'things will be all right on the night' with an accompanying lack of objectivity.

One remedy is to place the project checkpoints into the hands of an independent party who is outside of the project sponsor's/manager's sphere of influence. They can then conduct the measures objectively and also perform any 'rescue missions' as necessary.

2.3   Three key communication issues to get right

Type: Analysis

Checklist description

One of the keys to a successful project has to be communication. Communication doesn't mean just talking and sending memos. It involves listening and understanding. However, there can be negative as well as positive communications – not talking or consulting sends a very clear message to those excluded.

For a project to be successful, the communication traffic shouldn't flow up to the project manager and down to the project team. Rather it should flow at all levels. But it should be the project manager who ensures that communication is occurring and that communication is appropriate.

This checklist helps to identify areas where communications are poor or have broken down.

Checklist

Developers
- Are they still learning and keen to learn about actual working conditions for those who will use the system?
- Are they keen to understand the business perspective even if it is not put logically or consistently?
- Are they beginning to wallow in the technical details?
- Are they checking what the 'tame' business users are telling them with independent sources?

Business users on the project
- Are they a practitioner of those they represent in the business community (and not just managers)?
- Are they maintaining contact with those they represent?
- Are they ensuring decisions made in development sessions are communicated to their peers?
- Are they 'clamming up' due to lack of confidence in the technical arena?
- Are they becoming more influenced by the developers than by their peer group?
- Are they locked into 'we've always done it that way' or are they open to new ideas based on technology (e.g. using a workaround even after a system has been fixed or developed)?

Target users of the system
- Are they aware of changes to the way they will use the system to do their jobs?
- Are some of their favourite aspects of the job being preserved (e.g. they may like walking between buildings to deliver forms because they can have a 'fag' break at the same time)?

Finally, check the developer/business user development sessions
- Have time constraints limited the discussion so that:
  - the whole ground has not been covered?
  - exceptions have been ignored?

- error handling has been ignored?
- disagreements have been quashed rather than explored?
- Has 'group think' been established which:
  - quashes debate, discussion or disagreement?
  - ignores obvious flaws in the thinking or output of the group?
- Is there a strong character who:
  - the group can't ignore since the character is in a position of power and authority (usually the manager or senior manager)?
  - quashes all discussion or debate?
  - is skewing the results of the group as they try to accommodate or appease them?

Definitions/techniques

Storyboard prototyping – walking something through in overview mode on a whiteboard or OHP. This is typically done for a particular path through the system, e.g. 'I start here, then this happens, then that happens (and so on) until I end here.'

Next steps

The level and type of communications should be checked by the project manager on a monthly basis so that any emerging issues can be 'nipped in the bud'.

There are a number of techniques that can be used to maintain the communication between the project team and its 'customers':

- document review/sign-off at key points
- continuous feedback – involvement of users throughout rather than at sign-off points
- walkthrough/replay – show what has been learnt so far, e.g. scenarios, diagrams, screen and report designs etc.
- prototyping/simulation – gives a more concrete feel for the system
- storyboard prototyping.

2.4 How to cut a project down to size

Type: Analysis

Checklist description

At some point in the analysis phase of a project, a set of functions to deliver are established (see checklist 5.4 'System boundary analysis for requirements'). This can be analysed using the Pareto scoring to give a cost-benefit view of functions. See checklist 5.5 'Functional priority analysis: applying the 80:20 rule'.

However, even after these kinds of analyses, the list of functions marked for delivery can be too extensive and other filters may need to be applied to reduce the size of the project.

This checklist can be used to analyse functions for their inclusion or exclusion in the (first) delivery. By looking at the various dimensions of each function, some delivery options can be generated.

Checklist

Simplicity
It's easy to make a success of something simple. Therefore:

- Include functions which:
    - are clearly defined
    - add most value
    - can be applied easily to an organization.
- Exclude functions which:
    - have woolly or under-defined requirements
    - have low or undefinable value
    - users will struggle to use or will use rarely.

Level of quality
The price tag of the function can be altered by changing the level of quality expected.

- Various attributes of a function can be changed:
    - validation of data including allowing duplicates
    - level of error reporting
    - level of auditing
    - level of security (note the Data Protection Act requirements, however)
    - robustness
    - performance.
- Therefore there is the need to check:
    - what is the quality expected by the project sponsor(s)?
    - are they prepared to pay for that level of quality?
    - what level of quality will the project sponsor 'pay' for and what level of quality will they not 'pay' for?

Value assessment

- Determine what is the value of the function to the project sponsor by drawing up an urgency/importance quadrant and entering functions in each quadrant.

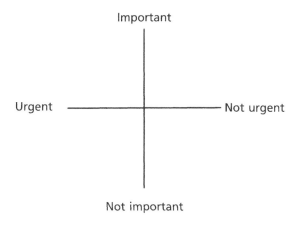

- Functions will fall into one of four categories:
  - urgent and important – need to do them now and get them right
  - urgent and trivial – need to do them now but they don't have much significance
  - non-urgent and important – need to do this sometime
  - non-urgent and trivial – don't need to do this.
- Ask the following questions about a function's value:
  - what if the function isn't delivered?
  - what is the function's contribution value to the whole system?
  - what other (lower cost) alternatives are there (i.e. deliver the business benefit some other way)?
- Note that 'value' is in the 'eye of the beholder'. Hence there may need to be several different value systems to identify functions which:
  - cause political difficulties or differences
  - have been included after a fight (i.e. a deal has already been struck)
  - are necessary but don't generate much enthusiasm.

Risk benefit assessment

Functions need to be costed in terms of their risk and value to the company. Questions can be asked of the system as a whole and of each individual function:

- Expenditure:
  - why should the money be spent on this function or system?
  - what is the ROI of the function or system? What are the alternatives?
  - what have we spent so far?
  - are we in line with budget or are there early indications of a possible budget overrun?
  - what are the budget milestones where we can detect overrun?
- Delay:
  - how long can we wait for this system or function?
  - what happens if we never get it?

- Size:
    - how complex will this system get?
    - how many business processes will the system affect?
    - what's the impact on the business?
    - can parts of the system be delivered that limit the impact?

Definitions/techniques

ROI = Return on investment = £ of perceived benefit/(cost of development plus cost of continued operation).

Next steps

The output of this analysis will be a list of functions falling into one of the following MSCW (MOSCOW) categories:

- must have day one (Must have)
- must be phased in (Should have)
- can be included at some point if there's time and budget (Could have)
- can be excluded (Won't have).

This can be used to define the plan for the detailed analysis and build phases of the project:

1   Establish first-cut timeframe and budget.

2   Produce first-cut overview of application concept (scope, i.e. what's in and what's out).

3   Set constraints – budget, time, resources, technology, compatibility.

4   First-cut project phases and sign-off points (deliverables).

2.5 How to avoid wasting time on things that don't matter

Type: To do

Checklist description

A project is comprised of a collection of tasks, targets, meetings, events and goals. Once a project has started, most of the management effort spent on these activities is to resolve issues and problems.

However, precious time can be spent on resolving issues and problems that, if evaluated, could be 'parked' either for the time being or indefinitely. Similarly, quite often, only the symptom is solved leaving the root cause unresolved.

This checklist helps analyse a problem before excessive resources are spent on solving it.

Checklist

Understand the problem
- What do you know about the problem?
    - does it always occur? What are the circumstances when it does/does not occur?
    - when/where is the problem most/least noticeable?
    - when did it first appear or become apparent?
    - when did it last appear?
    - when will it next appear?
    - is there a direct or most likely cause?
- What don't you know about the problem?
- What do you need to know about the problem?
- What are your major objectives in solving the problem?
- What seems to be most/least important aspect(s) of the problem?

Determine problem owner
- Is it your problem?
- Why do you want to solve the problem?
    - how will making this change affect other aspects of your project?
    - what would happen/not happen if you make this change?
    - what would happen/not happen if you do not make this change?
- Who needs to solve the problem more than you?
    - be careful of trying to solve every problem. Some problems cannot be solved with code (at least not without huge expense)
    - is it a personnel issue?
    - is it a training or communication issue?
    - is it a business process issue?
    - is it a supplier issue?
    - is it a political or ownership issue?

Assess problem significance: solve or not solve?
- Check the problem domain. Is it in-scope or out-scope for this project?
- Look at the big picture. How significant is the problem?

- Can it be left, ignored or eliminated by a different approach at a high level?
- What would happen if the problem was solved?
  - what will it cost to fix it?
  - what wouldn't happen if the problem was solved? What will be the benefit or saving if the problem is solved?
- What will happen if the problem is not solved?
  - what will it cost if the problem is not solved?
  - what will change over time? Will it get better or worse?
  - will the cost of not solving the problem get higher over time?
  - how long can you leave it?
- What will not happen if the problem is not solved?
  - what saving or benefit would be missed if the problem is not solved?

Sanity clause: test your assumptions
- What assumptions are you making:
  - about the causes of the problem?
  - about the effects of the problem?
  - about the owner of the problem?
  - about the importance of the problem? Where does it fit in the whole scheme of things?
  - about the urgency of the problem?
  - are you sure you are looking at the problem and not the symptom of a more basic problem?

Definitions/techniques

None.

Next steps

There are three potential outputs from this exercise:

1   Ignore the problem (too small, not yours to solve etc.).

2   The problem is we don't know enough about the problem to start solving it – need more low-cost research.

3   Solve the problem.

If the problem is to be solved, the checklist 2.6 'Different ways of generating solutions for a problem' can be used to marshall the appropriate forces to solve the problem.

2.6 Different ways of generating solutions for a problem

Type: To do

Checklist description

All project managers are required to solve a wide variety of problems. Apart from communication issues and personnel issues, problems often crop up in the system's design, build, and implementation. The problem is normally highlighted to the project manager and he or she is expected to chair the problem-solving exercise.

As a facilitator in this situation, project managers require a range of problem-solving techniques to employ as they see fit. This checklist indicates some of the processes and techniques that can be used in a problem-solving session.

Checklist

Identify those affected by the problem
Identify people who may need to be involved in the problem-solving exercise. In other words, involve those who:

- discovered or reported the situation/problem
- are involved/affected by the problem – both winners and losers in the current situation
- can affect the effectiveness of any solution – both positive and negative influencers
- are critical of the problem or proposed solution – are they a 'hidden' stakeholder?

Planning the approach
Before any solutions are generated, map out the solution space or framework. This shouldn't be used during the ideas and solutions generation process but it can be used to judge the ideas once generated. However, in the judgement process some of the assumptions behind the solution space may be challenged.

- Where is the best place to begin looking for solutions?
- What type of solution would fit?
  - what must the solution be able to do?
  - what must it prevent?
- What type of solution wouldn't fit?
  - what must the solution not do?
  - what must the solution not allow?
- How will you know when you have got the solution?
  - what do you want to move towards?
  - what do you want to move away from?

Generating solutions
Select one or two ways of looking at the problem from the list below. Keep good ideas even if they are not strictly relevant.
- Sequential:
  - where does this idea/problem naturally lead to?
  - what are the causes/effects of the problem?
  - what are the causes/effects of the solution?

- Linking:
    - is there a linked set of problems?
    - are any of the elements/causes of the problem similar?
    - can the problem be broken down into smaller problems?
    - what parts of the problem can you solve?
    - can solutions be linked together to solve the problem?
- Abstracting:
    - what is the principle underlying the problem? Is this a symptom or a cause?
    - is this a specific instance of a more general type of problem?
    - is there one main problem and a set of smaller minor issues?
- Categorizing:
    - what types of problem or things are we dealing with?
    - what types of solutions could be employed for each type?
    - do the sub-solutions when combined solve the whole problem?
- Holistic:
    - are we seeing the whole problem or just a part of it? What is the whole problem?
    - what does our intuition or gut feeling tell us to do?
    - is there a pattern here?
- Adaption:
    - has a similar problem occurred in the past and what was done about it?
- Modification:
    - what can be changed about the problem and what can't be changed?
    - can some of the assumptions or basis of the problem be changed to alter the likelihood or ease of solution?
    - input refinement:
        - what makes the problem hard to solve? What can be changed to make it easier to solve?
        - can the inputs or pre-conditions be changed or prevented that eliminate the problem?
    - output refinement:
        - can the outputs or goals be changed so that what actually occurs is not a problem?
- Magnification:
    - examine each piece in detail
    - which piece is the most important one?
    - is there a small, simple area to fix that will change the nature of the whole problem?
- Minimization:
    - what is the big picture?
- Substitution:
    - what if we replace X with Y or B with A?
- Rearrangement:
    - what if you change the order of the inputs that create the problem?
    - what if you change the order of the outputs required?
    - what if you change the order of the processes that create the problem?
- Reversing:
    - try looking at the problem – backwards, inside-out, upside-down.

- Combining:
  - force relationships between arbitrary ideas – if X and Y combined what new object, idea or solution would emerge?
  - bring in outside unrelated items or apparently wacky ideas
  - what's the absolute ideal or impossible dream?
- Attribute listing:
  - can each characteristic be changed or improved?
- Morphological analysis:
  - take variables of each attribute and see if the variations can change the product when re-combined.
- Analogy:
  - who else has this problem?
  - how do they solve it? (For example how does Mother Nature or someone from a different discipline or industry solve this problem?)
- Inverting:
  - how might we achieve the opposite of our goal?
  - if your problem is to maximize X, can you achieve it by minimizing everything else? Beware of false syllogisms.

Judging solutions

There are a number of techniques that can be used to judge the solutions. A major part of this exercise is to build consensus where consensus may not necessarily mean unanimity or agreement without reservations.

- Use Edward De Bono's six thinking hats to look at a problem and solution from six different dimensions together:
  - white – information. Is the information about the problem complete? Is the solution complete?
  - red – intuition and feeling. What is the gut reaction, intuition, emotional view of the solution? What do you like/dislike about the solution?
  - black – logical negative. What are the problems with the approach, the negatives or disadvantages?
  - yellow – logical positive. What are the advantages of this approach, the positives or good issues?
  - green – creative. Ignoring implementation issues, how interesting are the ideas and possibilities?
  - blue – control of the thinking process. How do we do the problem-solving process? Are we going about this the best way?
- Use a majority-vote group technique:
  - get the group to develop judging criteria for the ideas
  - get each member to score the top N ideas on a scale of 1–5 (5 = highest rank)
  - total the scores for each idea – highest score is consensus idea (take a vote on shortened list if necessary).
- Use a risk-benefit approach to rank solutions:
  - is there a solution with obvious merit, an obvious candidate for success?
  - which solution can be salvaged if it is wrong?

- least investment
- good fallback position
- not all or nothing
  - is the timing right for each of the solutions?
    - is there a short-term, medium-term, long-term solution?
    - do the costs and timescales associated with each solution make one or other a clear winner?
    - does a 'quick 'n' dirty' solution prevent an ideal solution being deployed in future?

Plan the idea into reality

Having a solution and even having the right solution are no use if you have no way of implementing the solution. For any potential solution, there also has to be a plan to implement it. Go through the process of planning by answering the following questions?

- Do you have what you need to implement the idea?
  - have you got the right skills?
  - have you got the right people?
  - are there any other individuals who can help?
  - what's your strategy for getting what you need?
- What is the motivation to succeed?
  - does everyone share it?
  - if not, how do you get it across to everyone?
  - are you prepared to commit fully to this idea despite the inevitable setbacks?
- Are there costs or risks involved?
  - are you/others ready for this? Is the end worth it to everyone?
  - if it fails, have you got a back-up plan that can be activated in time?
  - how will you know if it is succeeding or failing?
  - what is the measure? Who will judge when to invoke it and who has authority to do so?
  - what are the obstacles or criticisms of the idea and what is your response?
  - is the criticism guarding a stakeholder that you haven't included and planned for?
  - plan which arguments you are prepared to engage in, which ones to avoid, which ones you can lose gracefully for the greater good. (There is no point in saying your solution is ideal; be ready to admit the drawbacks and risks. Also be ready to stress the rewards.)

Definitions/techniques

False syllogism – false development of a rule based on faulty logic, e.g. all cats have four legs, all dogs have four legs, therefore all dogs are cats.

Next steps

Before the project manager gets into spending resources (time, people etc.) solving a problem, there are a number of steps which should be employed:

1   Conduct your own analysis of the problem – see checklist 2.5 'How to avoid wasting time on things that don't matter'.

2   Identify all those interested or affected parties.

3   Clarify what type of problem is to be solved and select the appropriate technique (from the above list, a hybrid approach or other technique).

4   Facilitate the meeting using the technique but don't be afraid to ditch the technique if something better appears.

5   If necessary, break the problem down into sub-problems and hold meetings to solve each piece rather than tackle the whole problem in one meeting.

6   Once the solution is outlined, make sure it is allocated for someone to:
   • write up
   • allocate resource
   • manage the implementation.

2.7 Setting up a document-naming standard

Type: To do

Checklist description

Most projects produce a large volume of documents. Quite often, many design issues, constraints and potential solutions reside in memos and emails rather than in formal documents. However, these documents are rarely brought together, and, even if they are, they are not catalogued sufficiently for ease of use. What is required is a document-naming standard that enables reuse.

The following standard has been developed for storing all documentation produced within a project. The naming is intended for use within an eight-character filenaming environment without any versioning software. If unlimited filenames and document versioning are available, these standards can be adapted.

Checklist

General filenaming
- A computer filename allows eight characters followed by a dot ('.') and then a three-character suffix.

Project lifecycle documents
- Project lifecycle documents can be identified as:
    - documents that are standard deliverables in the project lifecycle (e.g. Specifications of Requirements, Design, etc.)
    - documents that are expected to be changed and maintained over the life of the project (i.e. they are not just written and circulated once but revisited)
    - documents which will be formally agreed and signed off
    - documents where versions of the document are significant.
- All such documents to be classified as to their project lifecycle type (see below) where appropriate in the format 'TTxxxvNN.ZZZ' where the first two characters ('TT') show the type as per the list below:

Project Initiation Form	PI
Project Charter	PC
Phase Control Form	PF
Feasibility Study Scoping Document	FS
Feasibility Study Report	FR
Cost-Benefit Analysis	CB
Project Plan	PP
Outline Business Requirements	OB
Invitation to Tender	IT
Evaluation of Responses to Tender	ET
Detailed Business Requirements	DB
Outline System Design	OS
Detailed System Design	DS
Module Design Specification	MD

System Build Documentation	SB
Procedure Manuals	PM
User Procedures Manuals	UM
System User Manuals	SM
IT Production Procedures	IP
Module Test Plans	MP
System Test Strategy	SS
System Test Plan	SP
System Test Scripts	ST
User Acceptance Test Strategy	UA
User Acceptance Test Plan	UP
User Acceptance Test Scripts	US
User Acceptance Test Threads	UT
Training Needs Analysis	TN
Training Strategy/Project Charter	TS
Training Course Delivery Plan	TD
Training Course Papers	TP
Training Course Assessments	TA
Conversion & Data Take On Strategy	CS
Conversion & Data Take On Plan	CD
Conversion & Data Take On Procedures	CP
Implementation Requirements	IR
Implementation Strategy & Plan	IS
Project Completion Analysis Report	PA
End of Project Review Report	PE
Post Implementation Review Document	PR
Service Level Agreement	SL
Quality Assessment Report	QA
Prototype Evaluation Report	PT

- the first two characters could be replaced by numbers if sorting within a single directory is required, e.g. all project documents start 1x, all requirements documents start 2x
- three characters ('xxx') are to be used to identify the document and to ensure it is a unique name within the project. Note that if files are to be held within a directory specifying the project, this is not required within the file name
- two digits for a version number ('NN') and prefixed with a 'v' for version
- the three-character suffix ('ZZZ') should be the natural extension used by these types of file which for Microsoft Word for Windows documents is 'doc'.

Date-related documents

Date-related documents can be identified as documents which apply to the time of writing (i.e. they are not maintained or replaced) but form part of the history of the project.

All such documents should be labelled in the format 'AyymmddC.ZZZ' where:

- 'A' stands for document type:
  - E Email
  - M Memoranda

- – S Minutes where 'S' stands for Seconds (comes after Minutes as 'M' is already used for memoranda)
- – F Sign-Off
- – T Timesheets
- – P Progress Status Reports
- – Q Quality Progress Meeting Agenda
- 'yymmdd' is year, month, day (in this order to allow sorting)
- 'C' is the sequence letter (a to z) of the documents of this type written on this date for this project
- the three-character suffix ('ZZZ') should be the natural extension used by these types of file which for Microsoft Word for Windows documents is 'doc'.

For example, F001017a.doc would be the first Sign-Off document for 17 October 2000.

Definitions/techniques

None.

Next steps

It is recommended that each project has its own directory on a shared drive where everyone on the project (or associated with it) can read, write, and view documents.

This directory should be reviewed by the project manager once a week to ensure:

- documents are being created in it
- document-naming standards are being adhered to.

As modules are being produced, separate directories may need to be created to contain the code (e.g. '\CODE'). This could be a sub-directory of the main project documentation directory. Underneath the '\CODE' directory, there should be directories to cater for:

- development code (to unit test level)
- test-in-progress code (for system/integration testing)
- user-accepted code.

See checklist 2.8 'How do I manage a piece of software?'.

2.8 How do I manage a piece of software?

Type: To do

Checklist description

Software, we are told, is grown not built. But software grows quite differently from the growth we see in nature. Bits of software grow and then other bits are added on, then that grows until another bit is added on, and so on. Hence, rather than getting 20 developers to develop 100 programs and fit them together at the end of the build phase, seek to develop a 'stable core' to which other programs can be added.

The difficulty comes when the new program added requires changes to the 'stable core'. What happens to those developers producing programs that work with the old stable core? What happens if the stable core is actually live? What if this program is a customization for one client but will not be released to all clients?

This checklist identifies what is required to manage software to minimize the risk of getting the software configuration wrong.

Checklist

1   Establish a baseline:

   (a)   A baseline is a starting point from which all changes can be made and managed. To get a baseline, the following is required:

      (i)   There should be a list of all components. The components should include:

- all project documentation:
  - Project Charters and Plans
  - Business/System Specifications
  - Test Threads
- all software components:
  - programs and source code files
  - compiler
  - database load scripts
  - data files used in the database load scripts
  - server operating system(s)
  - network operating system and protocols
  - database management system
  - additional third-party server software (e.g. firewall, virus checker, performance management)
  - client operating system(s) and drivers
  - client application software (e.g. browser, WP package etc.)
- all hardware components:
  - server model(s)
  - server processor(s) model(s)
  - server memory modules
  - server peripheral devices – disk drives, printers, RAID devices
  - server ports (number and type)
  - network devices – switches, routers, hubs

- client model(s)
- client processor(s) model(s)
- client memory modules
- client peripheral devices – disk drives, printers, slot-in cards (e.g. network)

- a unique reference and version number. For certain types of component you may also need to augment the version with:
  - patch number
  - service pack release number (or if several applied, which applied in which order)
  - updated date.

(ii) Add to each component, appropriate configuration-sheet information:
- registry settings
- internal settings (e.g. language, date format, DB connection strings)
- input fields (and field types) expected
- other dependent software and hardware names, and versions.

(b) This configuration information should be contained in a single file or document. You may need to keep a separate file or document per customer configuration (or a master list per customer indicating what versions of each are installed).

(c) Create a release-directory. There could be a release directory for each configuration containing all the required applications or a master directory for common components and sub-directories for each customer variant.

2   Implement a strict version control process:

(a) This process should cover the following:
   (i) application software
   (ii) third-party software releases
   (iii) hardware upgrades.

(b) Application software should be controlled in the following manner:
   (i) Software should move between the following directories:

Source directory	Target directory
Baseline	Individual developer's working area
Developer's working area	Completed
Completed	Test build
Test build	Either pass or fail
	Note that if there are mutually dependent modules they should all be moved to pass/fail together
Fail	Developer's working area
Pass	Available
Available	Next release (per core and/or per target customer)
Next release	Baseline (or customer-variant baseline)

   (ii) A version numbering regime must also be implemented:
   - all software should be booked out with a new version number

- all software cannot be booked back into baseline with the same version number that is already there
- all software, third-party or otherwise should come with a revised configuration sheet.

3   Ensure the baseline is used:

(a)   Note that if a new baseline is created:

(i)   all developers should be notified if they are using any of the old baseline for unit-testing purposes, and they should upgrade to the new one immediately

(ii)   all testers should be notified:

- software should be checked that the version numbers for software coming from developers is not a version lower than the new baseline
- all the test threads should be rerun against the new baseline.

(b)   Due to the impact of a new baseline, it should be carefully planned so that:

(i)   it has minimal impact on the development environment

(ii)   it has been slotted into a gap in the testing phase (rather than force a rerun of tests).

4   Evaluate all changes:

(a)   Since changes will cause the above cascade of movements in the software, it is vital that these changes are controlled.

(b)   Hence all changes should be checked to ensure they are essential.

(c)   What is the impact on:

(i)   user requirements?

(ii)   hardware usage?

(iii)   software usage?

(iv)   system capability?

(v)   costs?

(vi)   timescales?

(vii)   operational situation?

(viii)   impact on archived and backed-up data? Can it be restored or recovered if the system is changed (e.g. change in peripherals, media, table-structure, validation rule)?

(d)   Need to filter out changes which:

(i)   are too expensive

(ii)   are trivial

(iii)   have a significant impact on timescales

(iv)   are beyond original scope

(v)   will cause operational problems.

Definitions/techniques

None.

Next steps

Configuration management is a complex process but there are some tools/techniques that can be used to ease the burden, namely:

- Employ a configuration controller – his/her role is to:
  - control the movement of software and the configuration to all the directories
  - know exactly the status of individual software/hardware components
  - he/she should be selected carefully for this crucial task (i.e. this role should not be given to someone just because they are 'spare').
- Use a configuration-management tool:
  - there are a number on the market intended to assist in the production of software
  - however, not many can be used to control non-application elements (e.g. OpSys versions, registry settings etc.)
  - be careful on whether deltas are allowed (i.e. a piece of software can be booked out to more than one programmer at a time).

3
Business analysis checklists

3.1 Nine key questions for high-level business understanding

Type: Analysis

Checklist description

This checklist can be used to give a high-level, strategic view of a company and how it operates. It could be used to understand the company's relationship to internal and external factors.

A separate study should also be made of the company's relationship with its customers (see checklist 'How well do we serve our customers?').

Checklist

Look at the industry

1   What are the barriers to entry?

(a)   Are the set-up costs high or low (e.g. assembly line machinery vs network server)?
(b)   Do patents exist to prevent entry?
(c)   Do regulatory bodies protect the existing market?
(d)   What is the level of innovation and product release in the industry?

2   How would you characterize customer behaviour?

(a)   Is it easy for a customer to change from one competitor to another? What makes it hard or easy?
(b)   Is there brand loyalty?

3   What are the characteristics of the product?

(a)   What benefits does the customer gain from the product? Do your customers sell your product onto others? What is the gain for the customers of your customers? Map out the value-added chain to find the end result. For example, if you're a power-drill maker ultimately you sell holes.
(b)   Are all the products across the competition essentially the same? Does the customer choose the product primarily on price, service, brand, or something else?
(c)   What are the alternative or substitute products? Are there products which deliver the same benefit to the customer under development (e.g. LPs vs CDs)? How quickly can new products emerge?
(d)   How is the product delivered? Is it through personal contact (e.g. shop, home delivery) or impersonal (e.g. into a bank account)? Are there innovations in this or other industries which may change the delivery mechanism (e.g. Internet)?
(e)   Is it or can it be 'personalized'?
(f)   Is the product subject to changes in fashion, legislation etc.? How frequent are those changes? Are you impacted by changes in population mix? How predictable are those changes? Can they be foreseen or are they sudden?

Look at the company's performance within the industry

4   How big is the market?

(a)   Is your market expanding or contracting?

   (b)   As a company, do you have critical mass in your industry?

   (c)   Is your company a big fish in a little pond or a small fish in a big pond?

   (d)   Is the market divided evenly among the competitors or are there some big fish?

   (e)   Is your company playing a niche role? Who else is competing in that niche? How easy is it for your niche to disappear, become obsolete or expand?

5   How would your company be ranked?

   (a)   Is your company in the top, middle, bottom quartile in terms of market share?

   (b)   What is the difference in size between your closest competitors (above and below your ranking)?

   (c)   What is the difference in size (turnover, employees etc.) between you and the market leader?

6   What are your company's assumptions about the industry?

   (a)   What does your company expect to happen within 12, 24, 36 months? Will new technologies be introduced? Are mergers/acquisitions likely?

   (b)   What do they not expect to happen? What could happen that would severely affect their business and how likely is it (e.g. introduction of telephone banking)? Test these assumptions.

Look at the company

7   What is the breakdown of cost within the company?

   (a)   For every pound of your company's turnover, do a pie chart showing percentage of costs:

       (i)   raw material (including acquisition cost, buying staff etc.)

       (ii)   inventory (including warehouse costs, stockroom staff etc.)

       (iii)   production (people, machinery, running costs)

       (iv)   distribution (van, postage, store front)

       (v)   administration (finance, management and directors, IT, HR)

       (vi)   sales (salesforce, marketing, advertising)

       (vii) profit.

   (b)   How does the split of costs compare with the market leaders? How does it compare to those ranked above/below your rank?

8   What is the company culture?

   (a)   Is the company structure a hierarchy or flattened? Is there a branch network, divisional/regional offices or one central office? What is the communication like across the hierarchy or network? Do people feel involved or is there a 'them and us' or 'head office/branch' divide? What is the pattern of autonomy – centralized/decentralized?

   (b)   What is the company attitude towards quality – in product? in service? in supplier relations? in employee relations?

   (c)   Are employees 'empowered' or is there a strong centralized decision making made by an individual or élite?

   (d)   How political is the company? Are managers/directors always competing? Who is the final arbiter? Who has all the power? Is that person highly influenced by one or two others? Are ideas and plans selected on merit, personality or power broking?

   (e)   Is there a clear strategic direction? Is it well known or muffled?

(f) Is the company an entrepreneur/innovator/early adopter or risk adverse/living on past glory/failure?

(g) What is the reward structure like? Are innovators and hard workers identified and suitably rewarded? Is failure accepted or punished?

9   What are the business assets of the company?

(a) What are the critical activities of the business? What activities must the company do right to stay in business? What must it not do wrong to stay in business (e.g. legal restrictions)?

(b) Is there a critical skill-set, knowledge/understanding, competency within the company? Is it replaceable, i.e. are your key people replaceable? How protected is your critical skills/knowledge from theft or damage?

(c) Are your critical competencies too rigid and stifle innovation?

(d) How well are you doing at your critical activities compared with competitors? What level of priority is given to the critical activities? Are they resourced appropriately?

(e) What isn't essential to the business but is done anyway for, say, convenience (e.g. accounting, IT-development etc.)?

10   What is the level of IT support for the business?

(a) What types of applications do you need? Which are standard? Which are unique to your business (are they competitive edge)? What could be bought in?

(b) Where are your application backlogs?

(c) Do you require cutting edge or stability? What level of technology risk can you accept?

Definitions/techniques

See checklist 3.13 'Lines of questioning for a business process'.

Next steps

This analysis can be used to:

- engender debate about the company's strategic position and direction
- draw up the parameters for a balanced-scorecard exercise
- identify a goal for a business review
- identify business process(es) which need further study (see checklist 3.3 'Fourteen common business problems – spotting which ones are yours').

A separate study could be made to investigate the company's relationship with its customers – see checklist 3.2 'How do we analyse our relationship with our customers?'.

3.2 How do we analyse our relationship with our customers?

Type: To do

Checklist description

Each interaction between company and customer is the 'moment of truth' defining the customer's single, lasting impression of the company. This impression determines whether they will remain your customer. This checklist shows how to conduct a customer-measurement exercise.

Checklist

1   Collect customer satisfaction information:
    - regular contact (sales/post-sales calls)
    - call-centre analysis (types of query, complaints)
    - repeat business
    - questionnaire/survey (careful on the psychology of this)
    - number of returns in warranty period
    - spread of returns after warranty period.

2   Set up some product or service quality indicators as follows:
    - determine the 5–20 factors where customer perceives failure in product/service
    - weight them according to how annoying the customer views them (some more severe than others)
    - on a week-by-week, month-by-month basis, count the failures, multiply them by the 'severity factor' and broadcast them internally so people can see how you are doing
    - the ultimate objective is zero across the 5–20.

3   Analyse the level of customer-aware activities across your area of operations. For each of the following, identify where the customer is delighted and, if you were talking to a customer, determine in which area they would like you to do better:
    - capacity forecasting – volumes, stock levels, operators/staffing levels
    - order capture – distribution channels, simplicity, opening times
    - pricing – value for money
    - purchasing – availability, lead times, payment methods (e.g. have-now-pay-later)
    - manufacture – quality of material, quality of assembly, tested
    - product – sufficiently featured, customizable, easy to install, easy to use
    - fulfilment/delivery – priority, order tracking, shipping method, shipping time/place assisted installation and training
    - problem solving – returns and claims handling, post-sales service, training, help desk, manuals.

4   How well do you keep up the quality of product or service? For each of the above areas, is the quality delivered at all points of contact with the customer:
    - consistent?
    - reliable?
    - repeatable?
    - ongoing?

5   What is the balance between customer demands and internal constraints? Use this table analysis to show visually the balance of a business process – how much does the customer get versus how much does the company keep? This can help show the conflicting expectations in a process and who 'wins'. If you prioritize them it may show critical failings that the company must solve and critical advantages to the customer that the company must keep.

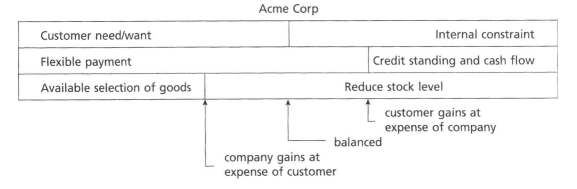

Acme Corp

Customer need/want	Internal constraint
Flexible payment	Credit standing and cash flow
Available selection of goods	Reduce stock level

customer gains at expense of company

balanced

company gains at expense of customer

Definitions/techniques

None.

Next steps

This analysis can be used to:

- identify a goal for a business review
- identify business process(es) which needs further study (see checklist 3.4 'Where business analysis usually goes wrong').

3.3 Fourteen common business problems – spotting which ones are yours

Type: Analysis

Checklist description

This checklist can be used to give a quick checklist of perceived business problem areas which can help to focus on which business processes should be looked at.

A 'voting' system could be used to rank the problems in order of significance:

Checklist

- [ ] Customers want goods faster than we can produce/deliver them
- [ ] If we could produce/deliver faster we can take customers away from competitors
- [ ] Our goods or services cost more to produce than our competitors'
- [ ] We cannot keep up to date with new technology or new practice, legislation, indussry code
- [ ] We lack customer focus or are perceived as being unresponsive to customer demands
- [ ] We take a long time to bring new products or services to market
- [ ] We lack innovation and are change resistant
- [ ] We don't have the know-how or drive to enter new markets
- [ ] We have poor quality of pre-/during/post-sales service
- [ ] We have poor quality of product
- [ ] We have poor quality of delivery
- [ ] We have a skills or resources shortage
- [ ] We are bureaucratic and exercise too much control
- [ ] We hold too high/low stock levels (just-in-time vs just-in-case)
- [ ] We don't know how to match capacity/supply with demand/usage

Definitions/techniques

None.

Next steps

After the most significant perceived problems have been identified, the set of business processes involved should be listed. A likely 'starting candidate' business process can then be identified as an area for a more detailed study (see checklist 3.4 'Where business analysis usually goes wrong').

3.4   Where business analysis usually goes wrong

Type: Analysis

Checklist description

This checklist should be used in the planning stage of a business analysis to set the scope of the study. By quantifying the scope at each point, the focus and intensity of the analysis effort can be set in advance.

Checklist

1   Level of detail:
   (a)   Be careful of information overload. Look at your target audience – how much detail are they interested in? Stop at the point where information is below their level of interest.
   (b)   How much time have you got? Fix your level of detail to the timescale – you can always get the project sponsor(s) to commission a more detailed study.

2   Involving all the necessary business divisions/departments:
   (a)   Most processes cut across several organizational boundaries both internal and external (e.g. suppliers). Have you ensured that these divisions/departments are involved in the exercise?

3   Senior management buy-in:
   (a)   Don't rely on a 'thumbs-up' from the board/steering committee, go and talk to all the divisional/departmental chiefs individually. List their expectations. Map out where they welcome change. Identify the 'sacred cows' – the things that they don't want to change. Try to assess whether the 'sacred cows' are there due to ego, power or pleasure/interest. Are they doing this because the MD says so or are they genuinely pro-change?
   (b)   How much trust is there on the senior management team? Are they a 'team' or are they a set of competing individuals?

4   Clear, genuine goal:
   (a)   Is there a clear goal? Does it have a definable end state?
   (b)   Is the project goal genuine or is there a hidden agenda? Is there a difficult people issue which is trying to be circumvented by the use of BPR/IT? Some examples of agendas might be:
      (i)   to create a power base (through increased information, responsibility/ownership or authority)
      (ii)   to remove a power base (through dispersed information, responsibility/ownership or authority)
      (iii)   to prove someone else is a problem
      (iv)   to distance the contact between individuals who don't like/trust each other.

5   Using the right resources:
   (a)   Who are the key players in the project? If your project is to improve customer satisfaction, have you got access to them to (a) give an initial view, (b) review/approve the changes?

(b) Do you need to get an external view of your company, i.e. use management consultants, market surveyors etc.?

(c) Are you using personnel with high analytical ability – company strategists, IT analysts?

(d) Do you have key technicians who can apply their knowledge of new technology to business processes?

6 Approaching the project from the right direction:

(a) Most change projects are IT led – build, buy or update a computer system. Even if it's a business sponsor who says 'I want a new system', it will still end up an IT-led project. To change the approach, you need to get the business sponsor to say, 'I want to change my business process from this to that'. Once it's recognized that the project is about the business, then the approach will not just focus on IT. All sorts of other elements can be considered. You can raise the question, 'Is IT the best way to change that business process?'

(b) Is the basis of the project to standardize business practices? If so, be careful of the 'one size fits all' mentality. Customers expect choice and flexibility which can't be delivered by standardized business practices – build a framework not a cage. Variety not uniformity is the expectation.

(c) People are innovative, flexible, adaptable – computer systems are not. If you are trying to bring about change in the organization (not just rationalize a process) then people not technology should be the focus of the project. After all, software applications and technology can be recreated (by a competitor) but the knowledge, skill, 'personal touch' in your company can only be taken by your competitor if you upset your own staff and they leave. Changing the culture of your company is the hardest undertaking but it is also the hardest to copy with success. Hence it is a barrier to competitors and can therefore give you long-term gains.

Definitions/techniques

None.

Next steps

It is important to flag at a high level if you believe that some of these key understandings are not in place with a project underway. It is likely that the project will flounder at some point without these foundations. The project will then:

- drag on too long
- become quagmired
- cost too much
- be cancelled
- more dangerously, be implemented badly by an exhausted team
- be seen to fail such that everyone disowns it and it becomes a demotivation issue.

Once these issues are addressed, the study can then be planned and conducted (see checklist 3.5 'What are the steps to analyse a business process?').

3.5 What are the steps to analyse a business process?

Type: To do

Checklist description

Use this checklist (and the checklists underlying this checklist) to plan how to attack a business analysis project.

Checklist

1   Identify the business process for analysis – see checklist 3.1 'Nine key questions for high-level business understanding'.

2   Identify the goal of the business analysis – see checklist 3.3 'Fourteen common business problems – spotting which ones are yours'.

3   List the types of information required:
- what data do we need?
- why do we need it?
- when do we need it (what step in the investigation)?
- what filters will we apply to screen out unneeded data (not all information is worth collecting)?

4   List the sources of information required:
- Some possible sources are:
    - strategy, policy and planning documentation
    - organizational chart
    - process actors themselves (including who they call, email, memo and who calls/emails/memos them)
    - process actors 'in-tray', 'out-tray', 'pending tray'
    - document distribution lists
    - documented procedures and standards
    - job descriptions
    - quality manuals
    - existing systems documentation.
- List the mix of people/user to involve/interview – a matrix of:
    - level of involvement in the process:
        - dedicated – does the process everyday
        - casual – does the process on an ad-hoc basis
        - QA/authorizers
        - performance monitors (e.g. supervisor, accounts, personnel)
    - level of system use:
        - expert – full understanding of entire application
        - capable – full understanding of business process in application
        - simple – understands only their screen/report-set
        - simple report/query only
        - MIS complex query – possibly using advanced SQL/tool

- IT support
- computer operations
- customer
- customer's customer
- supplier.

5   Select the appropriate information collection method(s):

- Possible methods of conducting an investigation:
  - documentation (cheap to collect and analyse but could be inaccurate/out of date)
  - questionnaire (difficult to eliminate bias in the questions and answers – especially if the sample is small)
  - interviews and/or run workshops (may be subject to bias)
  - observation (what do they actually do versus what they say they do – gaps, key omissions, assumptions).
- Advantages of the various methods:
  - documentation is cheap to collect and analyse
  - questionnaires can be widely distributed and analysed
  - interviews/workshops can be used to get a consensus view and uncover hidden work practices
  - observation helps to record what people actually do against what they say they do. They can help uncover gaps, key omissions and assumptions.
- Disadvantages of the various methods:
  - documentation is seldom kept up to date and may contain many inaccuracies
  - questionnaires are difficult to construct without bias and leading questions. Also depending on the mixture of 'closed' versus 'open' questions, questionnaires may make further analysis more difficult, i.e. if the questionnaire has 'open' questions, people will respond with a lot of text which is difficult to synthesize. Similarly if the questionnaire is composed mainly of 'closed' questions, it may not be very revealing
  - interviews/workshops may lead to peer pressure and a 'group norm' which isn't what individuals do. Also time constraints on this collection method may mean critical parts of the process are skimped in the investigation. In addition memory lapses may lead to omission, over emphasis or problem creation.
  - observation may suffer from the 'Hawthorne' effect – by being studied individuals stray from what they actually do to what you expect them to do.
- Questions to ask of study method:
  - are we truly measuring what we want to?
  - can we replicate these responses later?
  - is our sample size big enough and not biased, i.e. representative of population?
  - how long will it take us to gather the required information using this method? Have we got enough time?

6   Select the most appropriate modelling method (dependent on goal) – see checklist 3.6 'What are the techniques for describing a business process?'

7   Conduct the study and produce the appropriate models.

8   Analyse the model against the goals – see checklist 3.9 'How to identify what's bad in a business process'.

9   Produce a set of recommendations.

Definitions/techniques

None.

Next steps

The recommendations need to be presented and agreed with the project sponsor(s). The next steps will depend on what is agreed.

It is at this point that the goal of the project should be reviewed. The goal, so far, has been 'To investigate' or 'To study ... and produce recommendations'. If a recommendation has been accepted, a new goal should now be set.

Alternatively, close the business analysis project and start a new one with a new goal. Starting a new project is the cleaner of the two approaches since it shows projects starting and ending with definable goals rather than one long, drawn out project that never seems to come to an end. Another advantage of this approach is that it enables project managers to assess required resources/skills in small definite clumps that last for shorter timescales – hence plans do not differ wildly from expectations. Similarly, it reduces investment-risk since project sponsors only commission 'next stage' projects rather than commission everything upfront (to a highly speculative budget).

The new goal and project should be set in business terms (e.g. 'Change Process X to include/exclude Y element(s)') rather than a request for a new computer system – use checklist 3.9 'How to identify what's bad in a business process' to test the new goal.

3.6   What are the techniques for describing a business process?

Type: Analysis

Checklist description

This checklist can be used to select an appropriate business process modelling technique.

Checklist

- Flowcharts:
  - Purpose – to show the sequence and iteration of actions in a process
  - Advantages – visual, easily understood
  - Disadvantages – misses out on a key aspect of a business process: people
- Deployment flowcharts:
  - Purpose – same as flowchart except there are swim-lanes to show which activity is done by whom
  - Advantages – visual, easily understood, shows the roles that people play
  - Disadvantages – often process is only described from one point of view
- Role–activity diagrams:
  - Purpose – similar to a flowchart except that they also highlight interactions between types of individual (e.g. a purchasing clerk sending a purchase order for approval to his/her supervisor). Business events are also mapped
  - Advantages – visual, easily understood, shows events and interactions
  - Disadvantages – often process is only described from one point of view
- Dataflow diagrams:
  - Purpose – describes process in terms of input, process, output. These can be strung together to show the flow of information/data/resources through a process
  - Advantages – good to determine data/processing requirements for a system
  - Disadvantages – not a natural way of conceptualizing a process, ignores the people factor
- Process–hierarchy decomposition:
  - Purpose – describes a process by starting at the top level and decomposing the process into sub-processes then decomposing those processes, and so on
  - Advantages – simple to understand and can show common processes
  - Disadvantages – as with all decomposition techniques, what is the stopping condition? Also it shows neither data flow nor interactions
- Effect–cause decomposition:
  - Purpose – lists the good/bad outcomes of a process and decomposes to the causes of those effects. Those causes are then the next level of outcomes which is decomposed for their causes etc.
  - Advantages – can be diagrammed, good technique for getting to 'root causes', ignores system/people/politics boundaries
  - Disadvantages – doesn't create a process framework for redesigning the whole process
- Structured English:
  - Purpose – to describe a process as a set of instructions in terms of: sequences (do/perform task then do/perform next task), branches (if-then-else or case-statements), iterations (do-until, goto, go back to)

- – Advantages – can describe complex calculations and business rules
- – Disadvantages – not visual, does not give a process overview: useful for detail only. Not easy to analyse for process flaws
- Decision trees, tables, cause–effect diagrams:
  - – Purpose – to create a lookup tree/table which contains a series of questions and gives the action required for all the combinations of answers
  - – Advantages – can cover complex business rules/logic and ensure action is done for all combinations, can be used to create programs
  - – Disadvantages – low-level logic technique, doesn't address people issues
- Objective decomposition:
  - – Purpose – starts with 'what is the objective of the process and how is this achieved?' This lists the sub-processes. Each sub-process is then used in turn as the next starting point for the same questions – 'what is the objective of this sub-process and how is it achieved?'
  - – Advantages – keeps the end objective in focus, can be shown in a diagram
  - – Disadvantages – sometimes difficult to know when to stop decomposing
- IDEF/ICOM:
  - – Purpose – builds up processes as Input, Control, Output, Mechanism boxes. For example, in an order-delivery process, the Input might be an order, the Control might be the business process rules for picking order items, the Output would be the order items and the Mechanism would be the warehouse staff
  - – Advantages – shows not only the process and what it uses but can also show some of the organization controls placed on it
  - – Disadvantages – not a natural way of describing the process: it misses out the 'interaction' element between people

Definitions/techniques

Decomposition – often called 'top-down' whereby a problem or effect is stated at its highest level and then broken down into its component parts. Each part in turn is then similarly broken down into its sub-components. This process is repeated until a suitable level of detail is reached.

Cause–Effect diagramming – a special set of notations which shows how to combine a finite set of inputs to produce a finite set of outputs.

Next steps

Use checklist 3.11 'Ways of picking a business-modelling technique' to determine which technique to deploy.

3.7 Four problems with business process diagrams and how to fix them

Type: To do

Checklist description

This checklist can be used to review diagrams for suitability to their intended audience. Each diagram should be tested against one of these four problems. For each type of problem, one or more solutions are proffered.

Checklist

1 Complexity:

   If the diagram is too cluttered, it ceases to communicate effectively.
   (a) Are you trying to describe several processes on one diagram or is the process extended or highly involved? Try:
      (i) splitting the process up into three-sub-processes – start up, main body, close down. Do an overall diagram for the three groups and then a 'child' diagram for each sub-process
      (ii) identifying common processes and create a 'child' diagram for these common sub-processes
      (iii) removing blocks of tasks which are concerned with a single calculation or activity – it should either be a general task, e.g. 'Do X', or shown as a sub-process on a separate diagram or described textually as an accompaniment to the diagram
      (iv) removing complex decision logic (many nested 'ifs') into a separate diagram or document. Record the activity as a single set of outcomes on the main diagram, i.e. don't show how to get to the results just list the results. For example, many factors go into a credit-granting decision but just show the options: grant full, grant part, refuse.
   (b) Have you too many roles or interactions? Try:
      (i) checking that you are using role ('the hats people wear') rather than job titles
      (ii) splitting the process up into phases which involve smaller numbers of interactions
      (iii) aggregating the roles especially where the interactions are similar in nature (e.g. reviewing/authorizing).
   (c) Have you too many events/triggers? Try:
      (i) splitting the diagram up into a diagram per trigger or event.

2 Different people and departments do essentially the same process in different ways:
   (a) Check why are they different – is there a good reason for it. If so, there are a number of alternatives:
      (i) allow for different branches on the same diagram based around departments or roles
      (ii) create a second diagram with the same process name and a subtitle of the other person or department.

(b) If there is no good reason for differences, go back to the objective of the diagram to determine a course of action:

    (i) if you are to looking for a best practice, record the best practice and manually annotate differences

    (ii) if you are looking for a historical record of the process – create a set of diagrams for each variant but group them together.

3   Showing the current computer system:

    (a) Does your diagramming technique allow for this? Most have some capabilities for this:

        (i) DFDs – it is implicit in the DFD that you have selected a view of the DFD, one of current-physical, current-logical, required-logical, required-physical. If you are capturing the current business process (the current-physical), choose names for the processes which denote it is being conducted by the current computer system, e.g. 'MIS-Produce Monthly Sales Report'.

        (ii) flowcharts/role diagrams – introduce the computer application as a role within the diagram with which a human operator interacts. Note if there are several applications used in a process then use several roles. Note that computers can interact with each other without human intervention (e.g. proposal system may invoke the credit-checking system).

4   Showing time delays:

    (a) Most process diagrams do not have methods to show the impact of time on the process – often the dimension you are trying to reduce in a process. Depending on the technique, time can be shown:

        (i) DFDs – use temporary stores to indicate queues/batches/in-trays

        (ii) flowchart – create a 'pending' state and insert as necessary

        (iii) role activity – use two interactions to show something sent and then waited to receive. Alternatively, use state points to indicate a wait followed by the trigger for the next action to begin.

Definitions/techniques

None.

Next steps

Rework diagram(s) as necessary. Once a set of diagrams are prepared, use checklist 3.15 'Checking the redesigned process' to test for consistency across the set.

3.8 Quality checks for a business process model

Type: QA

Checklist description

Use the following tests to determine whether a set of business process diagrams are internally consistent with one another.

Checklist

1   Completeness checks:
    - all processes and sub-processes have their own diagrams
    - all forms, standard letters, screen, and reports used in interactions are included as supporting documentation.

2   Naming checks:
    - process names – consistent throughout the diagram(s) (especially in GOTO calls and common sub-processes)
    - role names – consistent throughout the diagram(s).

3   Levelling checks:
    - ensure sub-process has trigger with the same name(s) as the calling process(es) so you know where it's called from
    - ensure sub-processes (i.e. perform then return to main process) are distinguished from 'next process' (GOTOs which are the next in sequence)
    - trace circular process loops (infinite GOTOs or sub-processes which call their parents).

4   Interactions completeness:
    - correct identification of method and content – not 'send form' but 'send form X', not 'contact customer' but 'request payment' etc.
    - transfer of responsibility – is there a transfer sub-process? Does the transfer of responsibility start a new process which may be inside/outside the scope of investigation? If so, is it marked as such?
    - is the initiator of the interaction identified? Are there any interactions without forms or letters? Are there any forms or letters without interactions?

5   State indicators:
    - check all key management states, handovers, authorizations are identified (by state markers – e.g. now require authorization)
    - check 'waiting' states are identified.

Definitions/techniques

None.

Next steps

Once the diagrams are in a consistent state they can be incorporated into a requirements document or used for further business analysis – see checklist 3.9 'How to identify what's bad in a business process'.

3.9   How to identify what's bad in a business process

Type: Analysis

Checklist description

Once a business process model exists, it is possible to review the model looking for key areas of improvement/change.

Using the following list will help to generate recommendations for change.

Checklist

1   Look at the process owner:
   (a)   Is there a clear process owner from cradle to grave? This can be identified by naming the process using its start and end states and getting someone to say they own the 'start-state-to-end-state' process. If no one owns it, there are several ways this can manifest itself:
      (i)   there are many goals in the process
      (ii)   many goals leads to a proliferation of roles or activities leading to a complex process
      (iii)   there are many roles in the process which are essentially internally (rather than customer) focused
      (iv)   when a problem arises, no one takes responsibility for it nor is anyone authorized to solve it
      (v)   no one can tell the customer when delivery will occur because they are too dependent on each other's role.

   If there is not a clear process owner, it is vital to identify an owner who is empowered to act across the whole process. This may mean restructuring the company hierarchy to stop it getting in the way of the process.

2   Look at the goal of the process:
   (a)   Is the goal self-evident from the process? If not, what are the activities which are consistent with the goal and which activities 'obscure' the goal?
   (b)   If the process has no goal, is it therefore redundant?
   (c)   Is there sufficient value in the goal to make the process essential to the company?
   (d)   Is the goal in line with one of the critical success factors of the company? If not, is the goal correct or is the process redundant?
   (e)   Are there activities which do not directly contribute to the goal? Are there activities which:
      (i)   are internally focused (e.g. authorizations, data capture)?
      (ii)   add little value?
      (iii)   are not customer focused?
   (f)   Are there roles/interactions which do not contribute to the goal?
      (i)   authorizations
      (ii)   information passing
      (iii)   add little value (e.g. extensive data capture which is not used).

(g) Are there ineffective activities (doing the wrong job)?

(h) Are there inefficient activities (doing the right job poorly)?

(i) If an objective-decomposition technique has been used, start from the bottom up to check that:

   (i) why is this done? Follow this up the hierarchy. It may show up that no one knows how a lower objective fits into the big picture

   (ii) for each objective ask what the target of the action is – if there is no target there may be a flaw in this aspect of the process.

If 'Yes' to any of the above, several actions can be taken to restructure the business process:

- remove the low customer value tasks
- move low customer value tasks to parallel threads
- remove low customer value roles/interactions possibly by empowering the main process actor
- move low customer value roles/interactions to parallel threads, e.g. do not wait for authorization before proceeding
- remove tasks that have no clear contribution to the overall objective.

3 Look at the length of the critical path:

(a) How long is the process? Is it too long? Is it too short (i.e. cut corners and lower quality)?

(b) Is there an interaction bottleneck where information is sent but takes a long time to return?

(c) Are all the interactions necessary or are some for information/authorization only?

(d) Is there a role on which many threads converge (e.g. a 'power base')?

If 'Yes', this may indicate need for:

- empowerment and ownership of whole process
- restructure company hierarchy to combine/eliminate roles
- reduce/remove batches/queues/in-trays
- additional personnel to be trained/empowered to act in a scarce/'overpowered' role.

4 Look at the value chain:

(a) Does the process have value for the customer? Is the value identified?

(b) How strong is the value chain? Do all activities add high value to the process?

(c) Is the effort expended on the process rewarded with a suitable level of benefit for the customer? Are there a high number of quality checks compared to the actual work that gets done?

(d) Are the quality measures/controls in the right place?

(e) Are there low-value tasks on the critical path?

(f) How much duplication of effort is there (e.g. rekeying customer name and address)?

(g) Is some data captured but not strictly needed?

If 'Yes', can low-value tasks be:

- eliminated?
- automated?
- combined?
- moved off the critical path?

5   Look at the supply chain:

(a)   Are there queues, batches, in-trays – where are the process bottlenecks?

(b)   Is there a resource bottleneck?

(c)   Do people have the right materials at the right time or do they have to stop and get them or wait before they get them?

(d)   Do people have the right information at the right time to perform their function or is there a lag?

(e)   Does the process require high levels of time contingency/stock/stand-by personnel to work?

(f)   Does this process prevent/delay other critical processes?

(g)   Are there enough people doing the processes covered by this role?

(h)   Are there too many people doing this role?

(i)   Is there an overlap of responsibilities which means duplication/redoing of work is inevitable?

If 'Yes', there is a need to reconsider the delivery of materials/information in the process. (See also checklist 3.16 'Business process redesign – power-tool #1 – partnering'). It may be necessary to review staffing levels and job descriptions but beware of taking away tasks that people find interesting and rewarding.

6   Look at process complexity:

(a)   Is the organizational structure making the process overcomplex?

(b)   Are there pairs of roles that continually need to keep in touch?

(c)   Has a process been previously structured so as to keep each task relatively simple for an 'assembly-line' set-up?

(i)   probably done to maintain a low-cost, unskilled workforce

(ii)   however handover costs may have increased

(iii) there is also an increased risk of error.

(d)   Are there too many exceptions and workarounds and 'personal workstyles'?

–   could indicate the process has been oversimplified in a previous job-design exercise.

(e)   Is there sufficient flexibility in the process to allow for customer preferences?

If 'Yes', a number of options exist:

- realigning company hierarchy to minimize interactions
- automation of tasks
- splitting task up into simpler sub-processes
- splitting task up into separate processes depending on some process-determined factor (e.g. customer-type, product-type, order-type etc.)
- redesign process around an agreed 'best practice'.

7   Look at the roles people play in the process:

(a)   You can conduct a WEAR analysis (see below). This may show anomalies such as

(i)   several different responsible/authority figures i.e. blurring – things may fall through the cracks

(ii)   authority with no responsibility – an information-only 'power base'

(iii) responsible with no authority – unempowered

(iv)   all other roles with no expertise – needs training.

(b) Be careful not to trust what people say on this – a manager may say he/she is responsible but not actually take action to show that he/she is.

8   Other factors external to the process itself that should be examined:

(a) Are there any economies of scale that could be utilized?

(b) By increasing learning or experience would we improve the time, cost, volume or quality?

(c) Do we recognize our pattern of customer demand and do we supply accordingly?

(d) Do we deploy our internal resources to best effect? Are there pools of skills in another department or division that are underutilized?

(e) Are there external technologies that we could deploy? Are we early or late adopters?

(f) Is our geographical location good for our suppliers, our customers, both or neither?

Definitions/techniques

WEAR analysis – produce a matrix of roles (on the top axis) and actions or tasks (down the margin axis). For each role or action write whether the role is the (W)orker, the (E)xpert, the (A)uthorizer, the person (R)esponsible or a combination of all four.

Next steps

Produce a set of recommendations for review and acceptance – see checklist 4.4 'What documents should I produce?'.

3.10   Clarifying the business goal

Type: Analysis

Checklist description

In order to approach the business analysis from the right angle, it is important that the goal of the analysis is clear. Each of the following questions should be answered prior to selecting the business analysis approach.

Checklist

1   What level of change is expected?

   This is essentially a question of scope for the investigation. It is easy to over- or under-estimate the level of questions to ask. This is also a highly political issue where everyone's understanding of the level of change should be checked and double-checked.

   - Strategic – where anything is up for grabs
     - a top-down approach is needed
     - need to ask lots of questions about the company's mission/goals
     - what are we actually trying to do? Why do we do this? What if we don't? What else could we do? Why don't we do that?
   - Tactical – where specific business processes are identified for a rethink
     - understand a business process
     - who owns the process? What's the goal of the process? Who does what?
     - see checklists on business process analysis.
   - Operational – what to do when problems arise in a process
     - understand the nature of the problem
     - where did the problem originate? Whose problem is it? How do we fix it?
     - see checklist 2.5 'How to avoid wasting time on things that don't matter'.

2   For a tactical level of change, are there some obvious business processes to start with? There may be areas which are well known to the business which exhibit one or more of the following characteristics:
   - Problems/exceptions occur frequently causing severe disruption.
   - Activities appear chaotic or occur at random.
   - There is a recognized 'hornet's nest'.
   - There is a high impact on customer satisfaction.
   - A competitor has a distinct advantage.

3   If there is a specific (set of) business process(es) that are requiring analysis, what is the expected outcome?
   - There are various outcomes that are desired in a business process analysis:
     - improve or increase productivity, throughput or volume (i.e. speed or volume or both)
     - reduce costs
     - improve service or product quality (e.g. increase accuracy of data)
     - support complex tasks (or standardize them or enhance them)

 – expand sphere of operations (e.g. take on new tasks, products, or services).
- The exercise should set specific numbers against these and build in a measurement device in the new process or system.

Definitions/techniques

None.

Next steps

Once the goal has been made clear and agreed by all participating chiefs, the appropriate techniques can be selected and deployed – see checklist 3.5 'What are the steps to analyse a business process?'.

3.11 Ways of picking a business-modelling technique

Type: Analysis

Checklist description

It is important to employ a technique so that:

(a) it is understandable to the target audience
(b) it is understandable to those involved in producing it
(c) it it has the right level of detail
(d) it is a suitable 'launchpad' for the next step.

Analysing the techniques compared with the following dimensions can help to determine the best technique to use.

Checklist

1   What are the categories of techniques?
- High-level techniques:
  - objective decomposition
  - effect-cause decomposition.
- Detailed logic techniques:
  - flowcharts
  - deployment flowcharts
  - role activity diagrams
  - dataflow diagrams
  - state transition diagrams.
- Extreme detail techniques:
  - decision trees
  - structured English.

2   What is the aim of the analysis?
- High-level techniques can be used to:
  - understand why problems occur in a process
  - identify or revise the goal of a process.
- Detailed logic techniques can be used to:
  - gain an understanding of a complex process
  - rationalize a process
  - use as a basis for a 'quality circle' discussion
  - generate processing requirements for a computer system
  - generate data requirements for a computer system.
- Extreme detail techniques can be used to:
  - generate processing requirements for a computer system
  - generate data requirements for a computer system.

3   Who will use the model next?
- High-level business chiefs – use high-level techniques.
- Business process actors – use simple detailed logic techniques.

- Business consultants/analysts – use detailed logic diagrams backed up by extreme detail where necessary.
- IT analysts/designers – use detailed logic diagrams backed up by extreme detail when key business logic is involved.

4   How familiar is the business analyst with the technique?

- If the business analyst is new to the technique it's best not to field that analyst with that technique.

Definitions/techniques

Business process actors – the people who actually perform the business process.

Next steps

Plan how best to deploy the technique – in a group setting or individually – see checklist 3.6 'What are the techniques for describing a business process?'.

Determine what tools are required (a) whilst using the technique and (b) in the documentation stage.

3.12 Four key areas to a process

Type: To do

Checklist description

The purpose of this checklist is to capture a business process so that it can be analysed further. The emphasis at this stage is on recording what people actually do. Additional comments such as new ideas, requirements etc. could also be captured but it is probably best practice to steer away from redesigning the process until it is well understood.

This checklist is intended to help capture the 'current physical' elements of a process.

Checklist

1 Establish the goal of the process:
   (a) What is the purpose of this process?
   (b) Is there more than one goal?
   (c) Does the goal change depending on who the role is?

2 Ask questions to describe the process using the following characteristics:
   (a) Inputs – those things used to produce the output, e.g. a form, memo, letter or raw materials.
   (b) Outputs – the items produced from an operation or task, e.g. authorized/completed forms, subassemblies etc.
   (c) Operations or tasks – takes input(s), produces output(s), normally with a time duration.
   (d) Repositories – where inputs are stored until used and outputs placed until needed (e.g. a queue, an in-tray, a bin) or final resting place in this process (e.g. filing).
   (e) Decisions (explicit such as questions or implicit such as branching based on intrinsic knowledge).
   (f) Events (explicit, i.e. outside the normal process flow, implicit, i.e. occur routinely, e.g. expiry date reached).
   (g) Process flow – sequential, parallel, loops.
   (h) Interactions – special type of operation between one or more roles: may be instantaneous or delayed (e.g. get approval by phone vs get approval by fax – best to show separate).
   (i) Roles – people conducting an operation. It's not their job title rather the 'hat they are wearing' in a process. For example, a call centre supervisor may also answer calls when all the operators are busy – they are acting in the role of call centre operator. A role may be carried out by an external party such as a customer, tax inspector, BACS etc.

3 Focus on what the person adds to the process:
   (a) What is the level of expertise required?
       (i)   identify key skills and knowledge
       (ii) breadth or depth of experience.
   (b) What key decisions do they make? How do they make them and what information do they need to make those decisions?

4   Highlight critical aspects of the process:
   (a)   Where are the quality controls?
   (b)   Where are the quality-measuring devices (e.g. failure counts, task duration, case duration)?

Definitions/techniques

See checklist 3.13 'Lines of questioning for a business process'.

Next steps

If the project goal is to perform requirements capture for a process further questions could be asked – see checklist 3.13 'Lines of questioning for a business process'.

If the analyst has all the available information and wants to analyse the process, use checklist 3.12 'Four key areas to a process'.

3.13 Lines of questioning for a business process

Type: To do

Checklist description

Depending on the goal of the investigation, there are different types of questioning approaches that can be adopted. This is a sample of the well-known ones.

Select the most appropriate question-set for the task in hand.

Checklist

1   Standard questions for business process capture (no requirements or redesign):

- What 'hats' do you wear in your job?
- What products, services, forms and information do you produce in your job each day?
- What causes you to produce these items?
- Where do you produce these items?
- What services or products do you use?
- What skills and experience do you need for your job?
- What training did/do you receive?
- What are the steps of each activity?
- What tools do you use for what?
- What would you do if tools were not available?
- Where is each tool used?
- How is each tool used?
- Why do you receive/deliver items?
- How do you receive/deliver items?
- Do you produce the items you deliver?
- What is your role after delivery?
- Whom do you work with? What are their job titles? What 'hat' are they wearing when you work with them? What do they do for you?
- Whom do you supply? Who is your 'customer'? What do you supply them with?
- Who supplies you? What do they supply you? When do you get these items?
- Who initiates the interaction?
- How is the interaction triggered and completed?
- What materials flow?
- Do your suppliers understand your wants and needs?
- Do you have to get a sign-off for things you do? Who signs them off?
- When do you go to others/your manager and for what?
- What meetings do you have each day and for what?
- What agreements are made in the meetings?

2   Assumption questioning – getting the reason behind what people actually say:

They say	You ask	Their response tells you
We always/sometimes do that	Why?	True/false constraints on their work
We never do that	Why not?	True/false constraints on their work
That never works	Why not?	Is there a secret block that could be removed?
We have to do that	Says who?	Identifies correct/incorrect process owner/stakeholder
We don't have to do that	Says who?	Identifies correct/incorrect process owner/stakeholder
Often/sometimes this problem occurs	So what?	Identifies how critical the problem is to the process

3   What? Who? When? Where? How? Why? Process analysis and redesign combined questions (can also be asked at a strategic level):

• What is being done? • Are there any exceptions and how do you cope?	• Why is it being done? • What happens if we don't do it?	• What else could be done? • Why don't we do that?
• Who is doing it? • Who is it being done with? • Who is it being done to? • What are the demographics – sex, age etc?	• Why are they doing it? • What is their level of skill/knowledge/experience/ expertise? • Who else do you involve and why? • What are the roles present?	• Who else could do it? • Why don't they do it? • What should their skills be? • Are they daytime/shift/ night-time?
• When are they doing it? • Daytime/shift/night-time activity • How often? • How long does it take? • How sporadic is it? • How time-dependent is it?	• Why then? • Why does it take that long? • Why that frequency?	• When else could it be done? • Why don't we do it then? • Can the sequence be changed? • Can it be done more quickly? • If it was done more slowly, would quality rise?

• Where is it being done? • Is it being done anywhere else as well? • How does its location affect tasks which come before/after it?	• Why there? • Are there any restrictions on why it is done there (e.g. hygiene)?	• Where else could it be done? • Why don't we do it there? • Can it be made more accessible? • Is it easy to supply data there? • Is it easy to supply materials/manpower there?
		• Are ergonomic factors suitable – heating, lighting, safety, etc.? • Is rebuilding/renovation required?
• How is it being done? • How much material, effort and information is used? • How much waste?	• Why that way? • What are the policy standards, legal requirements (e.g. safety)?	• How else could it be done? • Can the material, effort and information be reduced? • Can the waste be reduced? • Can the waste be reduced? • Can different materials or methods be used? • Why aren't different methods or materials used?

4   Requirements capture questions:

- What are your needs?
- What would you like to see happen (i.e. wants)?
- What would you like to avoid happening?
- Are there any plans for changes at the moment?
- What benefits do you receive from doing this work?
- What are the rewards of this job?
- What are the penalties when you make a mistake?
- What are your job priorities? Who sets them?
- What obstacles, frustrations and dissatisfactions do you face?
- What are the constraints of the job? What are you prevented from doing? Who stops you and why?
- What do you have now that you mustn't lose?
- What do you get now that you don't use or want (e.g. cluttered screen)?
- What would you not want?
- What would you change if you had the opportunity?

5   Gap analysis for generating requirements or confirming completeness of requirements:

- What are the current system good points? What are the current system bad points?
- In what way does the process fail to meet a goal, target, management expectation, quality standard, quantity standard, missed opportunity or benefit? (= the GAP)
- What is missing from the process which causes the gap? What should happen ideally?

- What is the requirement that will move the process further to the ideal?
- What is the impact of making this change on personnel, process, data, and technical service? What will change in what they do (i.e. instead of doing this, they should now do that)?
- Do all the requirements cover management expectations and goals? (I.e. even if you deliver all requirements for business processes, are there other expectations not covered by a business process, e.g. MIS?)
- Are any requirements missing or misstated?
  - Do these requirements cover what the existing system does?
  - Do these requirements cover what the existing system doesn't do that you want/ need?
- If we can do these new requirements, what difference will it make to you?
- What is the impact of the new system?
  - How will what you do now change with the new system?
  - Are there any knock-on effects for making the change?

Definitions/techniques

Gap analysis – basically a line of questioning to establish the gap between the current and the ideal.

Next steps

Select the most appropriate line of questioning based on the goal of the exercise and who the respondents will be.

3.14   How to choose between alternative solutions for changing a business process

Type: Analysis

Checklist description

As part of a business process investigation, several alternative solutions should be developed. Each solution should achieve the desired goal.

There should be alternatives which cover two or more of the following categories:

Price-based solutions:

(a)   Low-cost 'mini' solution – cheap and cheerful but delivers benefits in a short timescale.
(b)   Medium-cost 'saloon' solution – middle price and effective, delivers benefits in a medium timescale.
(c)   High-cost 'Rolls-Royce' solution – high price with all 'bells and whistles' but will take a long time coming.

Technology-led solutions:

(a)   Full new technology-enabled solution – high use of technology either developed or bought: normally applies to application software.
(b)   Technology reapplied solution – use of existing technology but with some modifications (e.g. adding website as a front-end to an existing application).
(c)   Non-technology solution – identifies what could be done to the business process itself without using technology: often the most cost-effective solution.

Back-stop solution:

(a)   Current practice 'solution' – effectively this is a 'do-nothing' solution which should be used for cost-benefit comparison.

With a set of alternatives, the following questions could be asked against each alternative.

Checklist

1   What is the cost of the alternative?

•   This should include:
    –   development cost
    –   implementation cost (e.g. training, new equipment, new stationery etc.)
    –   operation costs (support staff, licences etc.)
    –   cost of fallback, backup and contingency position.

2   What is the benefit of the alternative?

•   This should include one or more of:
    –   increased speed
    –   increased throughput
    –   increased product or service quality
    –   increased customer-perceived satisfaction
    –   decreased waste

    – decreased new product or service development lifecycle
    – increased flexibility
    – increased ability to tailor product or service to customer needs and wants
    – increased innovation
    – increased job satisfaction.
- For each of these there should be an estimate of 'by how much', i.e. 'how much increase or decrease?'

3   What are the implications of the alternative?
- There may be some non-quantitative implications of the alternative:
    – does it change company policy?
    – does it comply with legislation or standards?
    – what does it do to company culture?
    – what does it do to management style?
    – what does it do to staff motivation? How does it affect reward and punishment systems?
    – how does it affect the rest of the organization structures and people?
    – how will it be perceived in the organization?
    – how will it be perceived by the union?
    – how will it be perceived by our suppliers?
    – how will it be perceived by our customers?
    – how will it be perceived by our shareholders?

Definitions/techniques

See checklist 5.5 'Functional priority analysis – applying the 80:20 rule'.

Next steps

After analysing the alternatives, select the best alternative that matches the project goal. Produce a document which explains the 'new' process:

- How it achieves the goal.
- The detail of the actual process, answering the following questions:
    – how should the tasks in the process be performed?
    when should the tasks in the process be performed?
    – where should the various tasks be performed?
    – who should perform the tasks and at what points?
- Cost/benefit justification for adopting this solution.

See also checklist 4.4 'What documents should I produce?'. Finally, use checklist 3.15 'Checking the redesigned process' to verify that the solution is implementable.

3.15 Checking the redesigned process

Type: QA

Checklist description

Once a process has been analysed and redundant tasks removed etc. it is important to review the revised process to ensure that key features have not been overlooked. Changing business processes is never easy for those promoting the changes and for those whose role may change.

This checklist is a 'sanity check' to ensure that the changes proposed can be implemented and have the overall desired effect. It should be used prior to formally presenting your recommendations.

Checklist

1   Check the agent of change:
   (a)   Is the agent of change centred on IT, technology, processes and procedures or people?
   (b)   People are the real key to business change – they should be at the centre of any process change. The change should be desired by them not imposed on them. Involvement and communication can help to reduce the barriers to change:
       (i)   (fear of) loss of job
       (ii) (fear of) loss of job satisfaction
       (iii) (fear of) loss of 'voice' over job demands and expectations.
   (c)   Does the job empower people to make their own redesign contributions?
       (i)   changes should empower people to do their jobs and allow them freedom to meet customer demands as they arise
       (ii) it is important to build a framework not a cage. Give guidelines as to what people can and cannot do rather than 'just do this'
       (iii) customer satisfaction cannot be delivered from a rulebook which employees slavishly follow. Without the ability to meet changing circumstances, employees will feel demotivated and are not able to deliver the variety that the customer wants.
   (d)   The ability for people to discuss jobs with their peers may be the only change that is needed to bring about permanent change to a business process:
       (i)   people innovate not computers: a new computer system may not deliver as many benefits over the long term as a 'quality circle' that meets intermittently to discuss improvements
       (ii) IT, new procedures and policies should be seen only as tools to provide those on the customer 'coalface' with what they need to do their job and do it well.

2   Check the redesigned process against customer expectations:
   (a)   Does the redesigned process meet customer expectations?
   (b)   Are there any other parts of the process which can be redesigned at this point to meet customer expectations?
   (c)   Does the redesigned process exceed customer expectations? Can it be designed to give more than the customer is expecting?

(d) As customer expectations increase, can the redesigned process be changed to match them?

3   Check for oversimplification:

(a) This is a problem with the analytical approach. There is a danger of a 'one size fits all' mistake.

(b) A model is just a model and the real world can throw far more variety etc. than can be easily shown on a diagram no matter how well drawn or elegant that diagram/model is.

(c) It is important to check that this has not occurred in the redesign process such that the new process will not cater for real business demands. The well drawn diagram may not mean that the process has been well redesigned nor does it mean that it can be easily executed in the real world.

(d) A highly customizable product or service may need to be covered by several different business processes rather than one generic one which cannot be successfully implemented.

4   Check for missing the 'satisfiers':

(a) Different people have different satisfiers of a process – a manager may want good control but an employee may want variety and interest. Ensure that you know the different satisfiers of all those who have an interest in the change of the process and that their satisfiers are addressed. It may not be possible to satisfy everyone but it may be possible to 'trade' satisfiers.

(b) Make sure that different types of customer (with different satisfiers) are catered for in the process or define a business process for each type of customer (e.g. big manufacturing customer may want 1000 identical units of a product, a single customer may want one product to their own specifications).

5   Check that the redesign process is comprehensive enough:

(a) Are there any 'weak links' in the process? Is there a department or process that hasn't been covered? Don't forget every contact is the 'moment of truth' for the customer – they will judge the company based on its weakest link.

(b) Have you brought both your suppliers and your customers into the value chain? The interactions and delivery mechanisms between you and your suppliers and you and your customers need to be incorporated to bring radical improvement to a process.

6   Check the rate or degree of change:

(a) People can only adopt so much change before they suffer from 'change fatigue'. Communicate the overall plan but build in time for people to acclimatize to one change before another is brought in.

(b) Make sure that the length of the change process isn't too long or drawn out. When people get tired of change they become unresponsive to new changes and demoralized with a 'told you so' blame culture.

7   Check the 'big picture':

(a) See the change in the context of the whole organization – its culture and values, the relationship with customers, the relationship with suppliers, the relationship with employees.

(b) Be careful of process redesign becoming a cost-cutting exercise:

(i) cutting head count may cut quality – something which customers value. A cost-cutting exercise may turn into a throat-slitting exercise

(ii) cutting head count may result in losing vital knowledge, skills or capability. This may occur even if those key skills are not directly made redundant since layoffs are seen as a demoralizing act.

(c) Increasing the throughput may lead to a more tired organization not necessarily a successful one. There is a need to get people to work smarter not harder. People need to be invited to share creative or innovative ideas of how processes could be made more efficient or more effective. When they do this they should be rewarded rather than ratching up throughput again.

(d) Is the change part of a move to a new culture of improvement or will the organization adopt the new process as the 'normal way of doing things'?

Definitions/techniques

None.

Next steps

Some revision or reanalysis may be necessary before proceeding to get the revised process agreed by the business chiefs.

3.16   Business process redesign – power tool #1 – partnering

Type: Analysis

Checklist description

One of the most powerful process redesign techniques is to identify and utilize partnerships.

When analysing a business process, use this checklist to determine whether it can be radically changed using a partner.

Checklist

1   Who could we partner with?

Look at:
- suppliers of materials
- suppliers of services
- distributors
- customers
- niche-occupying 'competitors'
- mutual-product providers (e.g. wallpaper and paste).

2   What sort of deal could be forged?

Look for mutual advantages where a company could:
- gain a monopoly of raw material
- receive raw material in 'ready to process' state
- receive raw material at more suitable times/places
- deliver product in 'ready to use' state (especially if you are a manufacturer supplying to other manufacturers)
- deliver product at more suitable times/places
- gain more influence to determine industry direction hence opportunity to skew standards towards a company's current and developing products or services (e.g. promote safety standards when company already exceeds them)
- remove duplication of effort between the two partners
- engage in an initiative where participation of both parties will lower the cost for both partners (e.g. redesign packaging to fit redesigned shelf space).

3   What are the qualities of a good partner?
- right partner – is empowered, wants change/innovation, can bring something to the party
- right process – one that will benefit ultimate customer
- right people – people involved must be peers, positive, empowered
- right pitch – benefit must flow sufficiently (not necessarily equally) both ways to partners
- right follow-through – partnership must have a concrete plan with explicit deliverables and measurable benefits/success points, agreed timetable, team empowered to execute plan.

4   Effects of good partnerships:
- stymies competitors – once partnership is formed they cannot form it themselves

- keeps one step ahead of competitors – partnership often unanticipated by competitor
- creates barriers to entry
- can lead to further partnership initiatives
- can lead to a monopoly position.

Definitions/techniques

None.

Next steps

This kind of initiative needs to be thoroughly researched. It may need to be taken on by the business chiefs. However, the recommendation should be written up as part of the redesign process exercise – see checklist 4.4 'What documents should I produce?'. See also checklist 3.15 'Checking the redesigned process'.

3.17 Business process redesign – power tool #2 – IT

Type: Analysis

Checklist description

It is almost absurd to check the use of IT in businesses since it is often the first tool people seek to use in business change. However, often IT's role is relegated to supporting how the current process is conducted rather than bringing about any real change.

This checklist can be used to generate fresh ideas about the use of IT in a business process.

Checklist

Uses of IT:

- visualize a system before full development (see checklist 4.1 'Prototyping for requirements– the big issues')
- turn unstructured process into a structured one (and hence measurable)
- make processes work independent of location
- reduce or replace manual tasks including complex tasks (e.g. call centre, language translation etc.)
- capture expert knowledge to bring continuity of decisions (e.g. credit checking)
- bring relevant information to bear in the right place at the right time
- ability to present complex information in a more comprehensible format
- ability to determine hidden patterns of supplier, customer, market and company behaviour
- enables tasks to be performed concurrently rather than sequentially
- enables tracking and status management
- enables task duration and case duration to be captured and analysed
- can remove intermediaries
- can provide a 'self-service' mechanism
- can speed up communications to make some process almost simultaneous
- can be used as a distribution medium (e.g. for services, support, information)
- can be used as a customer behaviour feedback medium.

Definitions/techniques

None.

Next steps

If a new opportunity is identified, the recommendation should be written up as part of the redesign process exercise – see checklist 4.4 'What documents should I produce?'. See also checklist 3.15 'Checking the redesigned process'.

4
Business requirements checklists

4.1 Prototyping for requirements – the big issues

Type: Analysis

Checklist description

A real risk of business requirements capture is that it can be an extremely lengthy exercise – to cross all the 't's and dot all the 'i's. The risk is that users may be persuaded to accept that they want the set of proposed requirements through exhaustion. Business people don't know what they want until they can see they can have it – then they can't live without it.

Prototyping is a method for showing what a system will look like very early on in the development process. However, it is not without some potential for disaster.

This checklist can be used to determine whether prototyping would be a suitable technique for requirements gathering.

Checklist

What can a prototype be used for?
- simulation
  - to understand the implications of the system
  - identifies conflicts
  - allows alternatives to be tried
- requirements gathering
  - generates previously unforeseen needs
  - enables discussion about what the system should and should not do
  - tests desirability
- user involvement
  - encourages enthusiasm and interest
  - builds user commitment
  - establishes a confirmed starting point for development (e.g. screens, queries, reports can be 'fixed').

When to use prototyping
- 'look and feel' of system is difficult for business users to imagine
- data input/output requirements can be captured
- system is simple and straightforward
- to test a new software tool.

When not to use prototyping
- system is highly complex and needs extensive analysis
- user is too busy
- user will perceive prototype as finished (unless RAD approach to development is adopted)
- when everything requested in the prototype is expected to be in the final system irrespective of cost (i.e. what they ask for no matter how irrational or 'shopping list' is what they get)
- when 'having a computer system' is the first step in business process analysis.

Definitions/techniques

RAD – Rapid Application Development – a development method using an iterative prototyping to get better and better prototypes. The final version of the prototype is then deemed the working system. See checklist 1.11 'What sort of project lifecycle should I adopt?'

SystemCraft – a formalized method of RAD.

Next steps

If a prototype is appropriate then see checklist 4.2 'Six steps in a requirements-gathering prototype' for further information.

4.2 Six steps in a requirements-gathering prototype

Type: To do

Checklist description

The following is a method for conducting a requirements-gathering prototype. It is important that all those involved in the exercise agree certain rules:

(a) Prepare to move quickly – high-quality workmanship is not required at this point.
(b) Accept that your focus is the goal and nothing else.
(c) Be flexible and ego-less – your requirements may be recorded then sacrificed as unimportant.

Depending on the size of the prototype (and remember small is not only beautiful but necessary in this context), a team might consist of the following:

- 2–3 × business users
- 1–2 × business/systems analysts
- 3–4 × systems developers.

Any more than this and you may need to split the project into several prototypes or reconsider whether prototyping is the right approach.

Checklist

1 Identify basic needs:
   (a) What is the overall goal of the system? What need is it intended to meet?
   (b) Is there a set of objectives that must be achieved on the way, i.e. faster or slower, more or less throughput, higher or lower quality?
   (c) What are the limits/constraints? How much time and resource are you allowed to use? What can you change? What can you not change?
   (d) What sort of data needs to be captured and from where? (The less data and fewer sources the better.)
   (e) What sort of functions will be required? (The fewer the better.)
   (f) What sort of business users will there be?

2 Determine research questions:
   (a) What do we know already? What do we not know? What assumptions do we need confirmation of?
   (b) Is the level of quality and data accuracy known for each expected function?

3 Develop the primary screens and functions:
   (a) Use the developer's 'gut feel' for the first cut and revise with a business user.
   (b) Do not produce any ancillary functions (e.g. maintenance screens, login etc.).

4 Run a demo to all interested individuals:
   (a) Make sure you include actual users and business sponsors.
   (b) Run several demos if necessary to ensure all are included.
   (c) Pick up additional refinements and requirements through these demos.
   (d) Filter the refinements and requirements according to their impact on the primary goal.

5   Implement the selected new refinements and requirements:

   (a)   Update document of goals and objectives in line with comments from demo.

   (b)   Keep a list of all refinements and requirements that have been filtered out (for future use).

   (c)   Update primary screens and functions.

6   Continue with iteration until the only comments received would be 'filtered out' or until timebox deadline is reached.

Definitions/techniques

Time-box deadline – often prototyping is given a fixed timescale to capture as many requirements as possible. After the deadline has been reached no more requirements can be added – the system as defined at that point is then to be delivered (as the first version). Another time-box can be defined to capture requirements for the next release.

Next steps

There are a number of steps that could follow the above exercise:

- Requirements generated are reanalysed for completeness and consistency and this is then used to drive a full systems analysis, design and build process.
- Prototype is taken as first-cut system and is revised to give it 'build quality' and then delivered as first release.

An extremely key fact is not to deliver the prototype as it stands. Since prototypes are built 'on the fly' it may have a number of serious errors from a 'live' usage perspective. Normally prototypes exhibit one or more of the following flaws:

- little consideration has been given to performance and/or volume
- security and data-safety have been largely ignored
- lookup data for user choices and drop-down lists have not been fully captured
- background interfaces to other systems have been assumed but not built
- underlying data structures are ad hoc and will not easily support future enhancements to functionality (e.g. different customer addresses on different tables etc.)
- underlying module design is not architecturally sound and will be difficult to maintain (e.g. one module per screen even though there may be some common elements across screens etc.)
- there is no error checking in the code
- there is no data validation in the code.

For these reasons, it is best to allow developers to take apart the prototype and rebuild it to the final system. If prototyping has been accepted as the requirements analysis method, it must also be assumed that there is a build phase to be completed even after the prototype has been signed off.

The 'System build checklists', Chapter 6, contain more information on what to ensure is included in the build.

4.3 Easy things to miss in gathering requirements.

Type: Analysis

Checklist description

A question not often asked – 'what are the costs of an error in the Requirements Specification?' Errors in the requirements may have far-reaching effects:

- many components may be affected
- danger of overdesign
- may cause design complexity
- may cause design redundancy (unwanted features)
- may cause incorrect design – a flaw that may be difficult to remove.

This checklist is a 'sanity check' on the requirements to ensure that some of the 'harder to spot' issues are investigated. It should be conducted prior to Requirements Specification review.

Checklist

How might the use of the system change over time?
- Need to assess requirements in the light of:
  - learning curve
  - increased responsibility
  - staff turnover
  - performance pressures
  - rightsizing plus strategic direction
  - key man change (e.g. MD)
  - industry trends
  - government shifts, directives, legislation.
- How flexible would the system be to these changes? Are there any additional, 'long-term-view' requirements that should be added now to assist in the longevity of the system?

How would a system built on the requirements deal with 'real-world' issues?
No computerized system is perfect for a disorganized world – how would the proposed system deal with:

- incomplete forms
- the person who authorizes gets sick
- evolving processes
- abnormal, unexpected and unusual varieties of activities (non-standard jobs, emergencies)
- data that is ambiguous, uncertain, unpredictable or missing (e.g. missing post-code but system says its mandatory)
- data that can't easily be represented or analysed by a computer
- data that doesn't arrive in one lump but from several unpredictable sources.

Definitions/techniques

None.

Next steps

If there are no new requirements in the light of the above then the Requirements Specification can be submitted for review.

4.4 What documents should I produce?

Type: To do

Checklist description

Most business analyses assume that a new or revised computer system is the objective. To this end, most business analysis deliverables are aimed at producing 'Requirements Specifications'.

However, this kind of thinking leads to extremely large documents which try to cover all aspects of both the business and system requirements. These documents take a long time to produce, review and maintain.

Separating the business process changes from the requirements for a new or revised system will clarify what is actually occurring – a change to the business that is supported by IT.

This checklist can help determine what documents to produce, what should be in them, and consequently who the target reviewers and authorizers are.

Checklist

Business Process Specification

Purpose
To show how a business process can be revised for improvement. It also shows what changes will be expected across the business (including IT) to bring that improvement about.

It should be reviewed to ensure:
- recommended revision is the best option
- it is feasible in principle
- all departments and divisions can see and accept the impact.

Contains
- Business goal and investigation scope.
- Diagrams of current process(es).
- Analysis of current process problems.
- Description of revised process(es) including revised process diagrams.
- Justification of recommendation:
  - why change this and not that
  - why business should invest in this service (expected benefits over costs).
- Statements of expected impact on:
  - job roles and descriptions
  - organization structure
  - logistics
  - new and existing systems (both internal and external to the company)
  - system operations
  - supplier relations
  - employee relations (including unions etc.).
- Improvement measure for revised business process.
- Contingency if revised process does not meet improvement measure.
- First-cut timescale for both business and system changes.

Target audience
- Business users – to ensure current business process is correct and revision is feasible.
- Business analysts – to ensure impacts across the business are comprehensive.
- Business chiefs – to assess impacts and accept or reject change. This group is responsible for the next stage in the change process.

Next document
- If the revised business process is accepted then the business chiefs should commission an 'owner' to plan and manage the change process. This change process should encompass any existing or new system development plans when they are made.

Business Process System Interaction Overview

Purpose

To show how the users interact with the system at a high level. It is basically a translation of requirements into a set of key transactions. It should be checked to ensure that the business scenarios are:
- complete (i.e. none missing)
- realistic.
  Due to its lack of detail and technical jargon, this document is key in expressing expectations of the new system.

Contains
- Sets of business scenarios in a business process (including exceptions), e.g. Use-Cases.
- For each scenario, a description of how the user interacts with the system – what they do and what they expect the system to do in response.
- Different types of users and how they interact with the system including what their business process is. Note the interaction may not be the main process being revised – e.g. management reporting in an order-entry business process.

Target audience
- Business users (to ensure the scenarios are complete and realistic and to express what they expect).
- Systems designers/analysts (to understand what is expected of the new or revised system).
- Business chiefs (to monitor expectations and accept or reject how the system is intended to respond).

Next document
- Once the scenarios are complete and accepted, a detailed set of requirements can be produced. Note that scenarios and detailed requirements can be developed together but this document should be produced and accepted before detailed requirements can be finalized and presented for sign-off. If the scenarios aren't complete then it is not likely that detailed requirements will be complete.
- Note that scenarios are a powerful method for developing acceptance test plans, see Chapter 7 'QA and testing checklists'.

Detailed Business Requirements Specification

Purpose

To explain in detail what is required in a new or revised system from the business perspective – it should include needs, wants, don't wants, nice-to-haves. The document can be organized around business processes or screen-sets or other appropriate grouping. There should be no technical language within the document.

It is separate from the Detailed System Requirements Specification since the requirements captured are about how they do their job with the system – there are certain 'system require-ments' which systems design personnel will also 'build in' that are invisible to the business user (e.g. backup requirements) – see 'Next document' below.

Contains
- types of business transactions by types of user's matrix
- number of users by transaction types by user-types
- screen and report layouts (possibly produced from a prototype)
- business data items to be used (input/output)
- business data items sources (manual input, interfaces, batch runs, calculated etc.)
- business data input validations
- calculation rubrics
- legal, fiscal rules, standards
- business quality/throughput measuring devices (counts, statistics, start/end dates/times plus reports/queries of same)
- volumes by transaction-type
- priority value per requirement (indication of need, want, don't want, nice-to-have)
- identification of the type of user that has specified the requirement
- non-functional requirements (e.g. usability, level of help, training).

Target audience
- Business users (to ensure requirements are complete).
- Business chiefs (to accept or reject the requirements and to set their relative priorities).
- System designers (to understand what is required).

Next document
- All requirements that are 'invisible' to the business users should be recorded in a Detailed System Requirements Specification.
- It is often helpful to produce a cost-benefit analysis which can be used to drive the development plan (i.e. phase one to contain biggest benefit etc.). This can be used as a 'round two' review of the requirements to filter out any requirements which are high cost but low value – see checklist 5.5 'Functional priority analysis: applying the 80:20 rule'.
- Once the Detailed Business/System Requirements Specifications are produced, costed and agreed, a development plan can be drawn up and the production of the System Design Specification can commence.

Detailed System Requirements Specification
Purpose
To complement the Detailed Business Requirements Specification. This document contains the requirements that are technical or 'invisible' to the business.

Contains
- conversion of data or system including data cleanse, reformatting, handling of missing data, handling of historic data (see Section 8 'System implementation checklists')
- backup routines
- recovery routines

- contingency for catastrophic failure (per component – data, network, machine, batch job etc.) and disaster-recovery options (duplicate system configuration? replication? safe site?)
- system availability
- logon/logoff method
- logon control (including creating/disabling user access)
- password controls (encryption/decryption standards, method of changing)
- interfaces with other systems both inside and outside company – sales, accounts, engineering, manufacturing (method, timing, changes required to source/target system)
- interfaces with other new and planned systems
- how system should handle and check for duplicates (e.g. name and address, duplicate invoice etc.)
- data volumes
- overnight processing capability (and monitoring)
- ad-hoc reporting (e.g. system performance statistic, security logs, report logs, audit trail, Data Protection Act print)
- compatibility with existing hardware, op-sys, network protocols, DBMS
- impact on PC memory and network bandwidth
- impact on PC, network, hardware, disk configuration (e.g. new hardware or software required and will they fit inside existing configuration?)
- impact on disk space and disk controllers (i.e. system data size and backup-size – will they fit and can they be serviced by existing disks and disk controllers?)
- portability to other systems
- ability to tailor the system to individual and departmental preferences
- non-functional requirements (use of standards, level of performance, site changes).

Target audience
- DB/system administrators (to ensure completeness and feasibility).
- Business/IT chiefs (to accept/reject requirements).

Next document
- As per Detailed Business Requirements Specification.

Definitions/techniques

See checklist 4.2 'Six steps in a requirements-gathering prototype'.

Next steps

Once these documents are agreed, the System Design Specifications can be produced. Some work may have already commenced on these documents prior to completion of the Requirements Specifications.

See checklist 5.6 'Shortcuts to move from business process analysis to systems analysis'.

4.5 How good is my business requirements specification?

Type: QA

Checklist description

Apply this checklist to both the Detailed Business and System Requirements Specifications to determine whether they are suitable for review and sign-off.

Checklist

Overall check of the specification

- [ ] Must not be a mammoth list (with too much detail).
- [ ] Contains consistent not conflicting requirements.
- [ ] Contains consistent naming for business processes, events, triggers, forms, calculations.
- [ ] User requirements state what the user wants.
- [ ] System requirements state what the system must do in addition to user requirements.
- [ ] The users own their own requirements.
- [ ] Company critical tasks are met if requirements are met.
- [ ] Different types of users are catered for.
- [ ] Different types of customer are catered for.

Individual requirement check

- [ ] Requirement is uniquely referenced for future use.
- [ ] Requirement stands alone.
- [ ] Requirement specifies exactly one thing.
- [ ] All special terms defined.
- [ ] Unambiguous terms used.
- [ ] Requirement must be verifiable – can be tested objectively and have no vague generalities, e.g. 'ease-of-use'.
- [ ] Requirement must be necessary.
- [ ] Requirement within scope.
- [ ] Requirement must be realistic. Warning: performance, safety, reliability and availability requirements can turn a cheap system into an expensive one if applied too globally to the system.
- [ ] Requirement has an implementation priority attached (e.g. must have day 1, must have by year-end etc.)

Definitions/techniques

None.

Next steps

Once Requirements Specifications have been checked in this way, they are suitable for review and sign-off.

There may be some requirements which fail one or more tests. These have to be looked at in more detail to determine:

- can it be dropped?
- can it be modified to satisfy the QA criteria?

There may be some 'political hot potatoes' – requirements which are unreasonable but which the business is unwilling to drop (e.g. fixed deadlines, 99.99 per cent availability, real-time response levels for complex queries etc.). A number of approaches can be applied to deal with these:

(a) be sure it is an unreasonable requirement before proceeding to deal with it
(b) try to find the requirement behind the requirement – why do they want it? Maybe the real requirement can be delivered (i.e. modify the stated requirement to what can be delivered)
(c) produce a development and maintenance cost for the requirement to show why it shouldn't be delivered
(d) show the impact that delivering the requirement would have on development, support and other areas of the business and system
(e) try to involve others in the debate until reason appears
(f) register it as a serious project risk and get sign-off from all the business chiefs before allowing it to remain.

Occasionally, a business user will say, 'I don't care how you deliver it. My role is to tell you what I want and you need to go away and work out how to do it. That's not my job.' This is essentially a 'lack of ownership' issue. As a professional, sure of your ground, you may have to say, 'As a professional, I have done my job and it can't be delivered. So we now need to work together on what we can both do about it.'

Now and again the business user is not going to be satisfied. There's not a lot you can do about that. Either continue with the requirement until it is obvious to all parties that there is a problem (the 'take the money and run' approach – IT suppliers do it all the time) or refuse to budge and see what happens, or even more radically don't take the job (companies do this all the time if they don't want a particular contract).

5
Systems analysis checklists

5.1 What should be in a methodology?

Type: Analysis

Checklist description

This checklist can be used to determine if all aspects of the design process have been covered. It could be used to check a bought-in methodology (e.g. SSADM, SDM, HOOD etc.), or to validate a 'home-grown' methodology to ensure nothing has been missed.

Look at each element and examine if all the different aspects within each element have been covered by the method.

Checklist

1   Defining (the what and why):

   (a)   Defining the requirements (see also Chapter 3 'Business analysis checklists')

      (i)   capture business definitions – business terms, critical calculations, derived data
      (ii)   capture prototype screens and reports and what they do (include data validations)
      (iii) 'look and feel' issues – use of menus, icons, toolbars, function keys
      (iv)   may be based on old system.

   (b)   Defining the framework

      (i)   technical architecture (especially if constrained by existing architecture)
      (ii)   user base (types of users and types of usage matrix)
      (iii) volumes – throughput and response times.

2   Designing (the how – part 1):

   (a)   Conceptual design ('blue sky')

      (i)   major application functional areas and what they do
      (ii)   major interface areas (context diagrams and system boundary analysis).

   (b)   Logical design (workable)

      (i)   Logical Data design (ERD, TNF, CLDD, Classes)
      (ii)   Function design (Function description, Methods, Message Paths, DFDs and Process decomposition)
      (iii) Event design (Event lists, Use-Cases)
      (iv)   Function, data, Event xrefs (CRUD matrix, Access Paths, ELHs).

   (c)   Physical design (buildable)

      (i)   physical data design (denormalized, indexes, SQL-Views)
      (ii)   component/module design
         • coupling and cohesion
         • tiers
         • common modules
         • DB rules and procedures
         • transaction design
         • locking strategy
      (iii) on-line help

(iv) security

(v) backup and disaster recovery strategy.

3 Building (the how – part 2):

(a) Coding

    (i) standards

    (ii) commenting standards

    (iii) library and external modules usage.

(b) Configuration management

    (i) design specifications

    (ii) code

    (iii) technical environment.

(c) Documentation

    (i) user guides

    (ii) computer operator guides.

4 Testing:

(a) Different levels of testing

    (i) unit – single modules that the outputs are correct given their inputs

    (ii) system – the collection of modules within the system boundary pass each other the correct inputs and produce the correct outputs

    (iii) integration – the interfaces between different systems pass each other the correct inputs and produce the correct outputs.

(b) Generation of test scripts.

Definitions/techniques

Coupling – the way modules link together – their communication paths – what data they pass or share between them.

Cohesion – the contents within a module – single or multifunctional and, if multifunctional, how those functions are related.

Next steps

A 'home-grown' or 'bought-in' methodology may not have all that is required to cover all aspects of the development process. This does not mean that the methodology cannot be used. However, it may mean that the methodology has to be enhanced. The checklists throughout this book can be used to enhance your chosen methodology. See also checklist 5.2 'How do you make a methodology?'

5.2 How do you make a methodology?

Type: To do

Checklist description

One size does not necessarily fit all! Often development methodologies fit into the 'one-size-fits-all' category. However, each development project contains a mixture of:

- people with different design backgrounds
- people with different design abilities
- different project deadlines, budgets, priorities
- different quality expectations.

Hence the project manager or lead systems analyst/developer must apply his/her knowledge of techniques to produce a method for that particular circumstance, project, team or department.

But what are the ingredients used to make a method? This checklist helps to define project lifecycle components.

Checklist

1 Deliverables list (what to produce):

   (a) Contents list of all the documents (and their contents' lists) that are to be produced.

   (b) Include all critical diagrams or sets of diagrams.

   (c) Indicate who is responsible for the production of those documents, who reviews them, who signs them off.

   (d) Deliverables are typically attached to project milestones.

2 Deliverables dependencies (when to produce):

   (a) In most development projects, the system is produced in stages, with project deliverables feeding in one from stage to the next.

   (b) Show which deliverable has to be delivered before the subsequent deliverable can be delivered completed.

   (c) Note that this list of dependencies does not necessarily mean that one deliverable will wait for its previous deliverable before starting. However, it should be true that the prior deliverable is finished before the current deliverable can be finished. For example, logical design can start while business requirements are still being finalized but it shouldn't be finished and signed off before business requirements are finished and signed off.

   (d) Each deliverable dependency should have a 'control point' to determine if the deliverable is suitable for the next stage.

   (e) If produced as a simple block diagram, it can be used as a method 'quick reference' guide.

3 Technique guidelines to produce deliverable (how to produce):

   (a) For each deliverable there should be a specified technique (or set of alternative or complementary techniques).

   (b) The techniques could either be a 'toolkit' (use one of these as required) or a 'cookbook' (gather these ingredients and proceed through these steps).

(c) These guidelines can be put in the form 'input–process–output':

    (i) input – what source(s) of information should be used in this technique (e.g. previous documents or deliverables, user survey/interview etc.)

    (ii) process – the steps to follow to produce the output, i.e. the description of the technique etc.

    (iii) output – the format required.

(d) Guidelines can also include best practices, hints and tips, and general principles.

4 Technique QA checklist:

(a) For each technique, there should be a checklist that enables someone to 'deskcheck' the output so that it is:

    (i) complete

    (ii) accurate

    (iii) consistent

    (iv) conforming to standards

    (v) maintainable (the above normally guarantees this but sometimes, for example, a diagram/document can agree on all points but is totally incomprehensible to anyone other than the author).

5 Forms, templates and worked examples:

(a) Document templates and forms should be produced to keep the 'look and feel' of project records consistent.

(b) However, even when given forms or templates, people often fail to produce what's expected for lack of an example to follow – so produce worked examples of forms or templates.

6 Standards and conventions:

(a) These can be used to great effect to maintain consistency and allow people working independently to bring their work together under one umbrella.

(b) Some examples:

    (i) naming standards – documents, module names, table and column naming

    (ii) indentation rules in code

    (iii) source code versioning and history recording

    (iv) document layout

    (v) source code headers (e.g. module description, version number, last author and date, list of tables, list of called modules with their version numbers)

(c) Some standards may be aimed at specific deliverables whereas some might apply to all deliverables.

Definitions/techniques

None.

Next steps

To launch a methodology, you will also need to develop:

- Training plan – people need to be trained in how to perform the new method. It might be worthwhile looking at Section 8 'System Implementation Checklists' to determine what sorts of things need to be in place to introduce the new method.

- Conversion plan – some projects may be in mid-flight, are you going to impose the new method on them? Will individuals have to run two projects they are working on in different ways?
- Feedback procedure – if certain parts of the method are not working, you need to be informed. Methods can fall into lack of use all because one or two areas didn't work. Allow the methodology to grow where necessary. Develop a quality-circle mentality.
- Limit the scope – build a framework not a cage. Don't lock people in so tight to the method that new techniques or procedures or exceptions can't be handled. Embrace new ways of doing things.
- Release mechanism – as the method changes, how will you roll out those changes to individuals and to projects? Is extra training required? Do you need to refresh training at certain points?
- Quality vs timescale culture – have you allowed for enough time in projects to follow the method with the right level of quality? Do people understand the level of quality (not too much, not too little)? Are project budgets and timescales realistic using the method?

Finally, a method can only bring a certain amount of order out of chaos. It does not guarantee success – a 'fool with a tool is still a fool'. Don't count on a method to solve all your problems. There may be a people issue which, if solved, could have a far more dramatic effect on the quality of what is being produced.

5.3 Moving from current physical to current logical

Type: To do

Checklist description

Often in systems design, an analyst has obtained a diagram of a current business process to be turned into a system. However, the current process may contain all kinds of tasks which would not necessarily need to be incorporated into a new system.

This checklist can be used to rationalize the current physical flow of information into a logical view. It is based on the technique for doing this to SSADM's data flow diagrams (DFDs) but the same principles can be used on other similar process flow diagrams.

Checklist

Removal of redundant physical processes and tasks

☐ Remove any process or task which is concerned with the physical transportation of data, documents or information (e.g. 'send delivery notice to Accounts').

☐ Remove any process or task which is concerned with the batching of 'same-type' documents (e.g. 'Collect today's invoices for despatch to Head Office').

☐ Remove any process or task which is concerned with collating complementary documents which have come out of the same process (e.g. 'Collect mortgage form and direct debit mandate').

☐ Remove any task or process which is there to correct document handling or collating errors (e.g. 'If direct debit mandate is missing, do X').

☐ Remove any process or task which is concerned with storing information (e.g. 'Photocopy and file order').

☐ Remove any process or task which deals with how resources or information are input or output from a machine or computer (e.g. 'Enter batch header then batch lines').

☐ Remove any processes or tasks which create control information for checking later.

☐ Remove any error-checking processes or tasks.

Removal of redundant data stores and bins

☐ Remove any data stores and queues where information and resources are stored waiting for their next process (e.g. in-trays, pigeonholes, subassembly buckets etc.).

☐ Combine into one data store any data stores which contain the same data – where multi-part stationery is used – the different parts should not be shown as different stores even if they have different titles, e.g. order, invoice, picklist, delivery note.

Removal of redundant data, resource and control flows

☐ Remove any flows to now redundant processes or data stores.

☐ Remove or redefine any data flow into a process where that process does not use some or all of the data in the data flow.

☐ Remove or redefine any data flows which contain duplicate information.

☐ Combine any data flows which come from the same logical process and all go into the next logical process.

☐ Combine any matched pair of data flows into a single data flow, e.g. order header and order line data flows should be combined into a single 'order details' data flow.

Definitions/techniques

None.

Next steps

Once these adjustments have been made, the process can be redrawn to give the current logical process model.

Additional requirements (for the new system) can now be introduced. These additions should also be checked for similar redundancies (i.e. matches the same rules as above). Care should be taken that this system is not 'like the last system only better'. New requirements can be so fundamental in nature that a complete redesign is necessary. It would be development suicide to try to fit them into the pattern of the old system.

Once this has been completed, the required logical process model has been produced. This can then be used in the physical design process.

5.4 System boundary analysis for requirements

Type: To do

Checklist description

Not all requirements specified in a Requirements Specification can be delivered through the delivery of a new system. Hence before development commences, it's important to know where the system boundary starts and ends with respect to stated requirements.

This checklist is used to determine at a high level how requirements can be delivered.

Note that:

- The method is 'broad-brush' and hence detailed or time-consuming analysis is to be avoided.
- The analysis can be done on either a requirement-by-requirement basis or on groups of requirements (e.g. by business process or system function).
- If the analysis is requirement by requirement, an overall function significance can be given when the requirements are subsequently brought together.
- It is recommended that several analysts work independently and then draw together a consensus which can be presented to the business panel for further refinement and agreement.
- There are two main areas for analysis – system boundary and then, within that, functional priority.

Checklist

1 Each requirement should be categorized as follows:
   (a) Allocate a code to each requirement as to the ideal method of satisfying it, e.g. Business Process, New System name, Existing System name etc.
   (b) Allocate a system-function name to each requirement to indicate which function within the system would need to be developed or enhanced to deliver the requirement.
   (c) Likelihood of requirement being delivered with this method – high, medium or low, i.e. some measure of its feasibility. For example, if the requirement is a change to a bought-in system, the likelihood of change might be 'low'.

2 High-likelihood requirements will be implemented in the appropriate manner – some change controls may need to be raised for enhancements to existing systems.

3 Medium-likelihood requirements need to be discussed to determine what are the factors which influence the delivery of the requirement. Eventually, these requirements should become either high- or low-likelihood requirements.

4 Low-likelihood requirements are unlikely to be delivered via the optimum delivery mechanism. A number of options exist here:
   (a) Defer the delivery of the requirement (subject to management approval).
   (b) Deliver a workaround that does not compromise the ideal solution – i.e. change the requirement.
   (c) Deliver the functionality in a separate solution – i.e. develop the requirements of the

ideal solution which can then be expanded to be a new system (i.e. create a new project).

(d) Accept the functionality within the planned system – i.e. develop parts of the planned system but ensure it will never be reused: a standalone solution. This will keep the interface to a difficult area to a minimum and if a better solution arrives it can be 'plugged in'.

5   For low-likelihood requirements categorized (above) for delivery means that they fall within the system boundary (even if they are to become a separate project).

Definitions/techniques

None.

Next steps

The end result of this analysis will be:

- a set of requirements and functions which fall within the system boundary
- a set of requirements which require business process change
- a set of requirements which will require change control to be invoked for existing systems.

By allocating function names, the 80:20 rule can be perceived – are 80 per cent of requirements delivered in 20 per cent of the functions? See checklist 5.5 'Functional priority analysis – applying the 80:20 rule'.

5.5 Functional priority analysis: applying the 80:20 rule

Type: To do

Checklist description

This checklist is used to order requirements so that a 'pecking order' of requirements is identified. The analysis can be used to determine which functions should be delivered early and which can be delayed. This allows some kind of phasing plan for components of a system to be derived. However, it should be noted that component dependencies are not determined by the method so care should be taken about the contents of each deliverable (i.e. that each deliverable can stand as a complete system).

Checklist

1   There are six values which need to be assigned to each requirement or function:

- User perception
  - 5 – need/must have (a justification of these should be documented)
  - 4 – must not (a justification of these should be documented)
  - 3 – want
  - 2 – don't want
  - 1 – nice to have.
- Usage as a percentage of time per month (given that time is money) on a scale of 1–10 (some of the business process volumetrics could be used for this)
  - 10 – all the time
  - 1 – very rarely.
- Potential time saving on a scale of 1–10
  - 1 – little/no impact on job
  - 10 – eliminates job altogether.
- Function complexity (function points) on a scale of 1–10
  - 1 – data field on screen
  - 3 – screen and table required
  - 5 – several screens and tables
  - 7 – complex calculation
  - 9 – key system integration and handover
  - 10 – all of the above – tightly integrated with other systems.
- Significance count – add the values together for each significance factor that applies e.g. $8+4$ means that the function is legally required but also adds to customer satisfaction
  - 8 – legal requirement
  - 4 – increases customer satisfaction
  - 2 – contributes to significant income/direct-cost-saving over time
  - 1 – contributes to user satisfaction over time.
- System significance count – indicator to show whether function is a background essential function that cannot be easily 'added in' later:
  - 1 – essential.

2 The overall value for a specific requirement is given by the following equation:
- value = perception * (usage + saving) * (11 − complexity) * (significance + 1)
- This calculation will give a value between 16 000 and 2 for each requirement.
- Note that this is a simple measure for giving a spread of values for each requirement or function. In time, someone may come up with a more sophisticated and scientific method.

3 Requirements are now grouped between high value/low cost and low value/high cost. From this, some decisions can be made as to possible roll-out strategies:
- Note that the system indicator can be used for sorting the functions or requirements into two groups (with priorities within each)
  - essential functions that have to be developed upfront
  - non-essential functions that can be phased in depending on their relative values.

4 Do a Pareto analysis on the lists:
- Calculate the cumulative values
  - sum up the total value for all requirement or function values
  - calculate 80 per cent of the total
  - list all the requirements or functions in value-descending order (or by essential/non-essential category and then value descending)
  - produce a cumulative running total of values down the list.
- The Pareto boundary is where the cumulative total exceeds the 80 per cent of total value. In many cases this occurs when you are just 20 per cent down the list (i.e. 20 per cent of the total count of entries in the list).

Definitions/techniques

Pareto analysis – based on nineteenth-century Italian economist, Vilfredo Pareto, who noted that 80 per cent of Italy's wealth was owned by 20 per cent of the population. The relationship has been found to be true in many other fields. Although not necessarily always in strict 80 : 20 split, it can be seen that a large proportion of effects are normally generated from a smaller proportion of causes.

The basic technique is as follows:

1 Give a numeric value to each item under analysis (e.g. benefit score, unit cost etc.).

2 List the items in order of magnitude starting with the largest.

3 Calculate the totals of all the items and calculate 80 per cent of the total.

4 Produce a running accumulative total for the list of items.

5 Pareto indicates that the 80 per cent threshold will occur one-fifth (20 per cent) down the list.

Next steps

Some systems may not conform to the 80:20 rule – they may be more 80:40 – i.e. 80 per cent of the useful functionality lies in 40 per cent of the functions. Even this is a useful static to determine since it still gives a plan of attack for delivering benefits upfront.

It is key in this approach 'not to throw the baby out with the bath water'. Some functions may have low business benefit but are 'core' to the running of the system, e.g. error handling, restart/recovery, security and auditing are all functions that are difficult to build in later. Any 'benefits upfront' plan should add in the 'core' functions as a given in the first phase.

Note also that the calculation used is extremely simple and there should be some discussion with the business sponsors about the intended delivery order – i.e. don't base it on these statistics alone!

The output of this analysis can be used to drive the build and delivery schedule – see checklist 1.6 'Determining the big three – targets, timescales and budgets.'

5.6 Shortcuts to move from business process analysis to systems analysis

Type: To do

Checklist description

If there has been a business process investigation preceding the decision to develop a system, then the output of the investigation can be used to 'kick-start' the systems analysis effort.

Typically, business process descriptions and diagrams contain references to the following:

- roles – the 'hats' that individuals wear in a business process. Note that a single individual may wear more than one 'hat'
- interactions – how the roles collaborate to achieve the goal of the process or sub-process
- sub-processes – common processes that get invoked during the main process
- tasks – the things that individuals do to achieve the goal of the process
- triggers – events that occur that either start, change or close a process.

Each of these references can be used as an input in the analysis phase as detailed in the checklist below.

Checklist

Role
- identify a user access to system-functions matrix
- identify a user usage of forms and standard stationery (in later development stages this can be used to develop a user access to data matrix).

Sub-processes
- identify common processes invoked from several main processes
- identify processing sequence and likely layout of menus/screens
- identify 'GOTO' buttons/options
- identify structure of user manual (especially if on-line help is required)
- identify possible test threads.

Triggers
- identify system events
- identify possible queues and statuses
- identify 'do' buttons
- identify interrupts and what processes they invoke.

Tasks
- identify calculations required
- identify diary functions required
- identify at a high level what information is required

- identify some decision-support functions (from implicit/explicit case refinement)
- identify critical statuses – possibly required for reporting/progress tracking.

Interactions
- identify forms and standard stationery to use for data analysis (and hence data items required)
- identify forms and standard stationery for possible screen design for input and hardcopy output (e.g. letters)
- identify possible groupware functions – mail, queues, authorizations etc.

Definitions/techniques

None.

Next steps

By analysing each of the business process outputs, the inputs can be compiled into the Systems Design documentation.

The analyst must be careful not to assume that the outputs from the business process investigation are complete from a systems design point of view. The generated inputs must be checked for:

- completeness
- accuracy
- within the system boundary
- consistency.

In other words, can the system be built using what has been defined so far or are there gaps which the analyst must flesh out? The best approach is to assume that there are gaps and inconsistencies which the analyst must endeavour to find – they're in there somewhere.

See checklist 5.7 'What's in a system specification?' to see how the information should be recorded.

5.7 What's in a system specification?

Type: QA

Checklist description

For completeness, this checklist can be used to determine if all the appropriate information has been captured during the analysis and design phases.

Ideally a specification should not be longer that 40–50 pages. Any larger than this and it is difficult to keep consistent, let alone capable of being reviewed!

Hence, depending on the size of the system, several specifications may be needed for different areas of the system. For example, separate specifications could be produced for:

- system conversion
- data definitions
- on-line functions
- batch functions
- maintenance functions
- system operation functions
- description of the technical environment
- security, backup and disaster recovery functions.

The following describe which sections should be present in a document. Depending on the functions being described, some sections may have more content than others.

Checklist

Definition of System Boundaries
- what the system does and does not do
- what systems are input/output interfaces to.

Function Overview and Detail
- data flow diagrams
- data inputs/outputs plus processing logic (description, flowchart, decision tree or psuedo code)
- complex data validation
- exception handling
- process chains and functions (could be Use-Cases)
- define what is client and what is server
- define what is central and what is remote
- define what is on-line and what is batch
- check for duplicate checks including controls to prevent duplicate batch runs (e.g. 2x month-end)
- check for system security functions (including a master 'access' on/off switch).

Data Model Design
- logical (TNF) and physical entity models
- data items – attributes and domains

- tables – name, primary index, secondary indices, growth, frequency to optimize
- columns – name, size, optionality, nulls, integrity rules, foreign keys.

Data to Function Design
- Entity Life History, CRUD matrices
- query access paths including volumes and frequency.

Interfaces
- servicing level – instant, on-line batch, overnight batch
- technical mechanics (how do they transfer data e.g. protocols, media, media-format etc.)
- system software.

System Operation and Security
- operational routines – batch runs – frequency and sequence
- locking, user access, database protection
- auto-time-out on unattended terminals or sessions?
- DBA functions – optimize, housekeeping, checkpointing, transaction-log purge
- maintenance of system settings, parameters, lookup tables
- disaster recovery tools and procedures.

Reports
- list of reports including frequency, run-by-whom, number of copies, distribution list (para-meterized?)
- regular (batch run) and requested – also access to reports matrix.

Technical Description (including make/model/version and supplier)
- hardware – processor, printer, scanner, disk drive, tape drive, CD-RW, network, PC, PC cards
- software – op sys, DBMS, compiler, packages, comms protocols/managers
- consumables – disks, tapes, paper, stationery (pre-printed), cables, cable ends.

Glossary/Definitions
- the meaning of mnemonics on screens
- the meaning of system terms (if unusual or unique to the system or a particular inter-pretation of a business term or concept)
- cross references to business terms or concepts document.

Definitions/techniques

None.

Next steps

Most business applications are produced with this kind of information. Without this kind of information, system developments will occur in a haphazard fashion and will take longer to produce due to the level of rework required. Its quality is also generally lower than a system that has been properly thought through.

Sometimes this information is not captured formally but is contained in memos, emails and diagrams on whiteboards or slide presentations.

Even if the information is sketchy and scattered, it should be brought together in one place so that gaps can be identified. It is worth remembering that flaws discovered in the analysis and design phase are estimated to be a hundred times cheaper to fix than flaws discovered after system implementation.

For some checks that could be applied to this information see checklists 5.8 'General quality checks for a system specification' and 5.9 'Checking a logical design'.

5.8 General quality checks for a system specification

Type: QA

Checklist description

It is one thing to have a Systems Design document but that does not guarantee that the course of systems development will run smoothly. For a Systems Design to be useful to the developers, it must be:

- accurate
- consistent
- complete.

This checklist is intended to assess the quality of the Systems Design document.

Checklist

Design accuracy
- Is the system design simple (KISS)?
  - Simple systems degrade more slowly when maintenance and refinements are applied.
  - Does it match the business problem or process?
  - Is there any overdesign? Are there too many additional (nice-to-have) functions?
  - Are there any areas of the design which may be a cause for concern due to complexity?
- Has a single design concept been applied in all areas so that the system has an overall design integrity?
  - Have similar sub-problems been identified and solved in a generic way?
  - Are there any functions which stick out as not belonging to this system?
- Can more generic designs be used which allow future requirements to be incorporated?
  - Often the difference between hardcoding and use of codes within lookup tables
  - Are common processes identified?

Design consistency
- Have all requirements been cross-referenced to design statements?
- Is the naming of each function, entity and data item consistent? To standard?

Design completeness
- Have all codes got decodes shown (in appendices, say)?
- Is the sequence of screens or batch programs shown where critical or not obvious?
- Are there processes to check and report on the integrity of the system?
- Has a flow of each different business transaction through the system (showing common modules) been produced?
- Has the flow of data in/out the system been produced?

Definitions/techniques

KISS – systems analysts golden rule: Keep It Simple, Stupid!

Next steps

Of all the checks made above, conceptual integrity is the single most important feature of a system design. If this is wrong, the whole build process will be severely hampered.

It is possible to get away with an incomplete design if the conceptual integrity is correct since functions can be slotted in.

5.9 Checking a logical design

Type: QA

Checklist description

During analysis and design, a number of design deliverables are produced which form a Systems Design Specification (see checklist 5.8 'General quality checks for a system specification'). This checklist can be used to check that the work on each deliverable is sufficiently complete.

Checklist

General

- Is logical design inclusive of operating environment issues (batch job submission and control, printing queues, tapes, database management, login and security)?
- How well-thought out are the connections with other systems?
- Have security arrangements been included?
- Has archiving been considered? How easy is archiving in the data model?
- Has MIS reporting been considered? Do MIS tables need to be added to the data model?

Logical Data Structure (LDS)

- Are all 1:m relationships on LDS valid and in the right direction? Are there any 1:1 relationships? Why are they there?
- Are there any optional masters on the LDS? If so, why?

Normalized data – Third Normal Form (TNF)

- Are all data items in TNF (use of required screens, reports and LPOs)?
- In TN, do all the data items appear only once (except for the keys)?
- Check TNF for repeating columns, part-key dependencies, non-key dependencies.
- Entities sharing the same key have been merged (potentially).
- Are all foreign keys identified on TNF?
- Check TNF for operational masters.
- Are all flows labelled on DFDs and are these data items included in the TNF? Are the contents of these data items noted somewhere?

Composite Logical Data Diagram (CLDD)

- Do all relationships show optionality?
- How close are the TNF, LDS and CLDD to one another? Do you get the impression that there are 'two views' of the data?
- Is the Requirements Specification clearly reflected in the CLDD?
- Are the contents of the data items fully documented or are there hidden values or rules?
- Check there are no relationship 'loops' (i.e. entity1 is the master of entity2, entity2 is the master of entity3, entity3 is the master of entity1).
- Are the rules for each data item documented? Do they tie up with the ELH and process outlines?
- Is the data-naming convention reasonable? Is the data naming consistent? Also check for synonyms, homonyms.

- How complex is the data model? Is it easy to isolate parts of the system on the model? Is it easy to include/exclude options? Does it look right?
- Is mandatory data clearly identified?
- Is there any feel for volumes and size of data/records? Is this information incorporated in the CLDD to give a rough sizing?
- Is there an excessive use of flags/indicators in the design which could be inferred from the presence or absence of data/records? Why are they there?

Logical Process Outlines (LPO)
- How clear are the process outlines?
- Do the process outlines tally up with the ELH?
- Do the process outlines go down to data-item level? If not, how have they done ELH?
- Have business-critical processes been identified? Are the optional processes identified in the BSO (business system options)?
- Can the process outlines be programmed as they are, i.e. are they logical and clear (we will have to learn about the system from them)?
- Are common processes identified? Are there any date routines or calculation routines which have been missed?
- Is there a list of 'like-to-haves'?
- Are system parameters and global tables clearly identified? Is the impact of a parameter or parameter table change discussed?
- Has each LPO been checked or walked through with the business analyst and/or department head? Was there a meeting of minds or a rubber stamp?
- Is the evolution of each process and data item detailed? If not, it is difficult to know the impact of certain design decisions and change impact is very difficult to assess. (This is especially true of status flags, common processes etc.)

Entity Life Histories (ELH)
- Are the ELHs based on real or logical events?
- Does the entity require a delete at birth to ensure entity is empty?
- Are unexpected events catered for?

Data Flow Diagrams (DFD)
- Data flows balance between levels.
- Levelling is appropriate, i.e. not too high level, not too detailed.
- Data description exists for each data store.
- Process descriptions exist for each process.
- Process shows what goes in contributes to what comes out.
- Data flow names are meaningful and not repetitive.
- Are all the inputs necessary for each process?
- There are no time dependencies shown on the diagram.
- There are no internal data stores which are only sources of data or sinks of data.

Definitions/techniques

Data sources – data stores which only provide data but never have data stored in it.

Data sinks – data stores which are only used to store data but the data is then never used anywhere.

Synonyms – things that have different names but are the same thing, e.g. clients and customers.

Homonyms – things that have the same name but are different things in different contexts, e.g. income. Is that net or gross? It may depend whether this is a tax system or a mortgage-assessment system.

Next steps

Make the revisions as necessary and reapply the checks.

See the checklist 5.7 'What's in a system specification?' to determine how to structure this information into a specification.

5.10   Six steps to first-cut data requirements

Type: To do

Checklist description

All business systems manipulate data of one sort or another. In a number of prototyping approaches, the analysis of the data is a secondary function if it is thought about at all. However, data is the bedrock of most business systems. Get the data design correct and the processing of the data easily follows. Get the data design wrong and the processing becomes laboured often requiring frequent rework to add in 'just another data item'.

This checklist is intended to focus some analysis effort on what is happening to the data in a required new system.

Checklist

1   Look at the (business) process model:
  - The business process model shows some of the entities and data as:
    - contents of forms, letters, email etc
    - data which drives decisions (i.e. if X then do Y)
    - results from decisions
  - Use the above to flesh out sets of data items to support these needs.

2   Determine required inputs:
  - Examine the data items from above and determine:
    - which can be derived from others, i.e. derived or calculated data?
    - which must be supplied to the system via
      - manual capture (through screens)?
      - system interface (another system providing data)?
        - What format is that data?
        - How is that data grouped?
        - When/how can it be collected?

3   Determine required outputs:
  - Examine all the forms of existing output to ensure all data required has been input from somewhere:
    - reports
    - screens of all types – input, query, search etc.
    - forms, letters, emails.
  - Examine all the forms of desired output to ensure all data required has been input from somewhere:
    - reports
    - screens of all types – input, query, search etc.
    - forms, letters, emails.

4   Determine data usage information:
  - In the new system:
    - which users input what data and where from (screens, reports, forms)?

- which users obtain data and where from (screens, reports, forms)?
  - how often – hourly, daily, weekly, monthly, yearly?
- what should be the response time of each type of use (seconds, hours, days)?

5 Define relationships between the data sets:
- Organize data into common or logical groups.
- Determine if any of that data within each group can be used to identify an item in the group (e.g. invoice number can be used to identify all the information to do with a single invoice) – this is called a 'natural key' to the data.
- If there is no 'natural key', add one (e.g. on a customer record, the customer name cannot be used as unique so add customer number).

6 Define the formats of the use of the data:
- How to capture it:
  - typical business transactions.
  - logical groups of screens.
- How to get at it:
  - logical sequence of menus/screens.
- What does it look like?
  - number of reports and screens depending on type of user or type of usage (e.g. balance sheet and trial balance reports).
  - grouping and layout of data on screens and reports.
  - use of short codes and abbreviations versus long descriptions.

Definitions/techniques

None.

Next steps

Having captured a first-cut impression of the data and its intended usage, it's important to pay attention to the structure of the data (also known as the database definition).

The structure of the data will determine how simple or difficult it is to access the data and whether the data stays consistent whenever displayed. For example, if you capture a customer's address on an order and separately capture the customer's address on an invoice, which address do you use for delivery?

See checklist 5.11 'How to do data modelling'.

5.11 How to do data modelling

Type: To do

Checklist description

Knowing what people do is only one part of analysis. Knowing what they manage is another. This leads to data modelling. Data modelling typically involves three things:

- Entities – real things that exist and about which a company must keep records.
- Attributes – facts about the things.
- Relationships – rules for co-existence and operations between the things, tells us relationships between things.

Data modelling can get quite complex. The following checklist is only intended as a 'memory-jogger' guide. Further training in this area is recommended for those who have limited experience and who need to produce a 'rigorous' data model (i.e. one with few flaws in it). Note that there are many drawing/CASE tools that support this activity and, for ease of drawing and amendment, it's well worth obtaining one.

Use this checklist to build an entity relationship diagram (or class diagram if OO).

Checklist

Entities
- Write a list of all the real-world things (customers, orders etc.) that are to be referred to in the system.
- These are drawn as boxes with the entity name shown within the box.
- By convention, the entity name should be in the singular, e.g. Customer not Customers, OrderLine not OrderLines.

Relationships
- Draw lines to link entities that are related to one another.
- Annotate the lines to show cardinality and optionality.
  - This can be done with a variety of notations (e.g. crows-foot etc.) or by writing numbers at each end of the line as below:
    - $1:1$ = one-to-one, e.g. a ship can only have one current captain
    - $1:1+$ = one-to-one or more – a customer can have one or more orders
    - $1:0+$ = one-to-none or more – an order can have none or more deliveries
    - $1:m$ = one-to-many – a car has many sub-components
    - $m:n$ = many-to-many – a house can have many owners, an owner could own many houses
- Ask the following questions:
  - In one-to-one relationships – is this true over time? (For example, a ship can have more than one captain over time.)
  - In one-to-one or more – can both entities be created at the same time or may one exist before the other? (For example, can a customer exist before an order?)

- Since many-to-many (m:n) type relationships are difficult to implement in modern systems, insert a link entity in the middle of those kinds of relationship. Then redraw the links to be one-to-many from the original entities to the link entity.
- Be careful of circular relationships where grandparent (entity) has many parents and parent has many children and children have many grandparents. This indicates some faulty logic somewhere in the process or that there is a repeating-hierarchy type structure, e.g. employee may manage other employees. This is normally shown by a looping link from the entity to itself.

Attributes
- For each entity, write down what attributes are required to be managed in that entity.
- Some sources for this data might be:
  - screens and reports from old system or the new system prototype
  - forms and letters (current or proposed) in the business process(es)
  - data required by an interface system (either interface in or out).
- Be careful when basing this research on what is there currently – look at the new requirements to ensure all the items of data required to support the new business processes have been captured.
- Remove or rename any attributes which are:
  - synonyms – things that have different names but are the same thing, e.g. clients and customers
  - homonyms – things that have the same name but are different things in different contexts, e.g. income. Is that net or gross? It may depend whether this is a tax system or a mortgage-assessment system.

Keys
- For each entity, peruse its attributes looking for a natural key, i.e. an attribute or a combination of attributes that would make an occurrence in that entity unique. For example, Car Registration Number might make each entry in a Car entity unique.
- Typical combinations of keys might be sequence numbers or dates. For example:
  - on an order-detail entity, the key might be order number + order-line number
  - on an Airport Schedule, the key might be Flight-code, flight-date.
- If there are no natural keys, an artificial key might need to be added, e.g. customer-number is better than customer-name since names can be the same.
- For link entities (see above), the key is normally a combination of the keys from the two original entities. For example, a ShipCaptain entity which links the entities Ship, Captain might have the key Ship-Name, Captain-Licence-No.

TNF structures
- Once entity keys have been established, some further analysis is required to tease out any hidden relationships in the data.
- Hidden relationships will cause problems later in the process because:
  - it may mean that only one set of data is captured when more than one is required, e.g. if we just stored the ship's captain information on the Ship entity, we may not be able to show a history of Captains for that ship
  - if data is interrelated, there is normally some processing required to maintain the relationship. By not identifying the relationship early enough, we may miss out on a crucial piece of processing, e.g. if on an Orders Entity, there is a Part-Number and

Part-description. These two items are related and should probably be maintained together outside of the Orders entity.

- TNF (Third Normal Form) is a method for examining data relationships within entities in a three-step process to ensure the relationships within the data are as simple (normal) as possible.
- Examine each entity in turn, investigating its attributes so that:
  - repeating groups are removed from an entity and given an entity in their own right. This new entity may inherit the key of the original entity plus additional attribute(s) to make each occurrence unique, e.g.:
    - if Order entity has OrderLine1, OrderLine2, OrderLine3, then this should be split out to be Order and OrderLine entities with OrderLines having key OrderId, OrderLineNumber
    - if Ship has PreviousCaptainID and CurrentCaptainID, this should be split out into Ship, ShipCaptain
  - any data that does not relate directly to the whole entity key should be split out into its own entity with that part key as the new entity's key, e.g.:
    - for ShipCaptain entity with key ShipID, CaptainID with attribute CaptainName, then CaptainName should be extracted into a Captain entity with CaptainId as the key
  - any attribute that is dependent on the values of another attribute should be split into its own entity with the other attribute as the key, e.g.:
    - from above on the Orders entity with attributes Part-Number and Part-description. Partdescription should be removed and a new entity, Part, created with key Part-Number and Part-description as an attribute.
- Any new tables created through this process should:
  - have their relationships link lines redrawn to show their relationship to other entities (including their optionality and cardinality)
  - be examined in the same way to ensure that they too have simple (normalized) relationships.
- Combine any new entities created but which share the same key:
  - for example, say there are two entities PartDescription with key PartNumber and data PartDescription and PartStock with key PartNumber and data QuantityInStock then these tables should be combined into entity 'Part' with key PartNumber and attributes PartDescription and QuantityInStock.
- The old tables should be removed from the diagram and the replacement tables should have their relationships link lines redrawn to show their (inherited) relationships to other entities (including their optionality and cardinality).

Definitions/techniques

Cardinality – simply 'to give a number to', 'to quantify'. In the entity context, it shows for one given entity how many of another entity may be related to it.

Next steps

Whilst the above exercise has, hopefully, captured all the data that is required for business processing, this is not the end of the data modelling process. The following should be added to the model for completeness:

- 'Physical' data items
  - these are additional attributes required to conduct the system processing, e.g. status-codes, created and updated time stamps etc.
  - these attributes should be collected and added to the model as the systems-design phase progresses.
  - note that they too must be normalized (see TNF above).
- DataTypes
  - each attribute should have a data type added. The data type indicates how it will be stored on the database.
  - by assigning the data type, some restriction is applied to the values allowed for that attribute:
    - integer – only whole numbers are allowed
    - date – only a valid date is allowed
    - character/string – combinations of letters and numbers are allowed
    - float – numbers with a decimal point are allowed.
- It is key that when assigning a data type, a data size is also specified, e.g. integer, smallint, float8, char(12) etc. Consult the DBMS technical manual to determine what data types are legal for that DBMS.
- Domains
  - a domain is a meta 'data type'. In other words, it adds more validation onto an attribute that is assigned to its domain.
  - some typical domains might be:
    - currency – where the number of decimal places is fixed
    - per cent – where the number of decimal places is fixed
    - english-date – where the format may be fixed to dd-mmm-yyyy
    - sortcode – where the format is fixed to NN-NN-NN
    - postcode – where the value will be validated against a list of known postcodes.
  - Common routines can be written to enforce domain validations to ensure consistency in data capture across the entire application.

For further data modelling and physicalization see checklist 6.1 'What logical data models get wrong (and have to be put right)'.

5.12 Object orientation – development steps for a data-centric approach

Type: To do

Checklist description

There are many formal Object Orientation (OO) methods in the marketplace. As with all formal methods there are many useful techniques but most developments do not have the luxury of time to use all of them.

The following checklist could be used as a less formal OO approach. It would suit small or pilot projects.

Checklist

Identify objects, attributes, methods and associations
- Possibly using verb-noun analysis of requirements or using techniques such as 'Use-Cases' (see definitions below).
- Discovery can be by spotting:
    - roles – individual or group conducting certain tasks within a process
    - interactions – both between people and between people and items or document (e.g. send invoice to Accounts)
    - events – things that happen in a process – initialize process, change process, end process
    - items and documents – invoices, orders etc.
    - places – warehouses, telephone exchange etc.

Categorize objects
- Association – an object 'has an' object. e.g. a car has (4) wheels.
- Inheritance – superclasses and subclasses. Superclasses may be abstract, i.e. no actual instances of it will exist, e.g. vehicle (abstract). Subclasses are generally concrete, e.g. a car (concrete) is a type of vehicle (abstract).
- Aggregation – where an object is made up of a number of others (e.g. train made up of engine, carriages etc.). Here the assembled class is often sent messages and it then sends delegate messages to its components. This is where polymorphism fits in (e.g. 'record' to a tape machine will then be sent to each relevant subcomponent in it which will do different tasks).
- Collections (i.e. a group of objects handled as a group, e.g. a list, a queue and hence group-handling methods – get next, get last).

Distil the design
- Eliminate any redundant or overdesign objects:
    - objects which are all function and no/little data
    - all data and no/little processes (except set and get)
    - objects which are only used by one other object – probably need to merge the two objects.

- Identify importance of each object (as a plan of attack – getting the most working in the least time).
- Identify the volatile objects or collections, i.e. what are stable definitions and what are subject to requirements change.

Analyse attributes (properties)
- Domain information – data type, allowable values, min/max, accuracy.
- Dependency information – other values, set of values, list of allowable values.
- Derivable – these should be left in during analysis and designed out if performance is not held to be a problem (but they should be identified).
- Type of unit, e.g. length in centimetres, inches, miles etc.

Reiterate analysis
- Look for more generalizations and opportunities to use inheritance. Note that as attributes are moved up a class hierarchy some of their methods may need to be moved with them.
- Look for areas of under- or over-design especially specializations where generalizing would lose some important details.
- Has proper attention been paid to high importance objects?
- Are there any classes that are effectively the same thing? Typically they share many common attributes – merge them.
- Follow the normal TNF rules for keys to objects.
- Check that the associations are valid and at the right level within the hierarchy (e.g. vehicle must have wheels – what if it's a boat?). Check also minimum-of-one links are at right level (e.g. customer must have at least one account – what if customer is only a prospect?)
- Are there any messages that pass through an object without significant change to that object?

Analyse state transitions
- For each object:
    - describe state
    - describe which events, attributes and links lead to this state
    - describe what events and actions change this state and to what.
- Produce a network of states – this is effectively a message or method path and identify hotspots by classifying each object:
    - passive objects – receive message and respond to sender with return values.
    - active objects – receive messages and send messages to other objects.
- Identify the setting of states which may interrupt current message path.

Detect required methods
- Methods can be detected by determining:
    - are there obvious object-method candidates (e.g. employee object may have a 'produce P60' method)?
    - what should be the object's response to each different type of incoming message?
    - what changes to an object's state are expected?
    - what are the 'real-world' events which might affect this object?
- Methods might fall into various categories:
    - primary methods (these are normally assumed to exist and are not normally shown):
        - create (includes validation beforehand)

- connect (establish relationship between objects)
- get (retrieve some values)
- set (update some values)
- disconnect (break connection and delete 'child' object)
  - problem or solution methods – object needs to do X, Y, Z
  - dynamic methods – object needs to respond to event A, B, C and generate event D
  - referential integrity – validation, error handling, time-out, synchronization.
- Look at stimulus and response for each objects and resolve any anomalies.
  - Are there objects that respond with no stimulus?
  - Are there objects stimulated with no response?

Apply methods and rationalize them

- Distribute methods to objects if the method primarily affects the object's attributes or state.
- After distributing the methods to 'likely-owner' objects – need to optimize the methods by checking:
  - methods that affect too many objects – the scope of a method should be limited to very few (ideally one) object.
  - if a method's sole function is to pass a message to another object's method, check if the design of the originating message is correct. Why does it use an intermediary object for message passing? Unless it's a polymorphism?
  - if a change in the response of one method affects the handling of the response in many other methods, there may be too much dependency in the methods. Consider consolidating some of the methods.
  - if many methods are invoked to achieve a single 'logical transaction' then maybe the chain of methods should be consolidated.

Definitions/techniques

Class – the definition type of an object.

Instance – a substantiated object – i.e. an object made 'live'.

Polymorphism – the ability of various objects to respond differently to the same message, e.g. print to an invoice object will be different from print to a cheque object even though the message is the same: 'print'.

Inheritance – the ability of an object to inherit code from a super-class and to provide code to a sub-class, e.g. 4-wheeled vehicle to car to Bentley.

State – the state of the object when encountered.

Messages – instructions to objects to do things.

Encapsulation – the ability of an object to hide what it is doing (i.e. black box).

Persistence – ability of an object to retain its state or data until the next time it is needed.

Property – a value that can be set or got from the object. Objects can have 'hidden properties' (aka private properties), i.e. properties that are hidden from the outside world declaration of the object but used by the object's own methods.

Use-Case – a technique to determine what objects a user might invoke in order to perform a business transaction. This is done by taking a business process and walking through how the user is expected to use the system to achieve that process.

Next steps

Object Orientated Design (OOD) is only a method for analysing the design of a system – it still has to be built. The techniques listed above should be used to produce a System Design document – see checklist 5.7 'What's in a system specification?'

Even with an OOD design specification, the build techniques needs to be determined:

- Will it be Object-Orientated Programming (OOP)? Or component based? Does the programming environment support OOP?
- What sort of architecture is expected? Is it client-server? Is the client thick/thin etc.? How many tiers exist in the architecture? Where is the application software expected to reside? Over how many servers? What is the network configuration – WAN/LAN/Internet?

See also checklist 1.11 'What sort of project lifecycle should I adopt'.

6
System build checklists

6.1 What logical data models get wrong (and have to be put right)

Type: Analysis

Checklist description

For most systems, the underlying database is the key to application-development success. Get the database structures right and everything else will normally follow. Get it wrong and chaos ensues as developers apply workarounds and temporary measures to get the application to work.

Often, the analysis phase can produce a pristine, logical data model. However, if the model is implemented without modifications, it can lead to a whole host of performance problems. The two main reasons to physicalize (or, more correctly, productionize) a logical data model are:

- speed/performance
- save space.

In preparation for this analysis, it is useful to list each entity with its attributes and mark each column as follows:

- Whether it is key to this or another table:
  - Primary (P)
  - Primary/Foreign (P/F)
  - Foreign (F)
  - Access Path or Secondary Index (A).
- Entity subtype indicator:
  - List the different subtypes for this entity (e.g. a customer could be a prospect or live and also a corporate or a consumer).
- Optionality of the data item:
  - Mandatory (M) – always present on every row.
  - Sometimes mandatory (S) – presence depends on the setting of another column – typical where there are entity subtypes, e.g. customer record may have forenames + surname or company-name depending on customer-type.
  - True optional (T) – may or may not be present.

This checklist gives some areas to consider in performing that exercise.

Checklist

1   Derived data:
- Identifying the problem
  - Seek out calculated values that exist on the screens and processes but not on any entity:
    - batch totals – amounts and counts
    - balance amounts – total amount due, total amount paid
    - statistics – averages, min/max values
    - status values
    - soundex keys.

- Resolution
  - There needs to be some assessment on the derived data based on:
    - how quickly it can be derived
    - how easily it can be derived.
  - If it is quick and easy to derive it then it should be derived on a 'as needed' basis using:
    - a single calculation module
    - an SQL-View of the data that includes the derivation.
  - If it is slow or complex to derive then the derived data should be stored on the database. This derived data will need to be maintained throughout the system using a single calculation module, e.g. an SQL-trigger that updates the derived field based on the update to one or more simple fields.

2 Large lumps of optional data:
- Identifying the problem
  - You may find there are large numbers of data items which are marked 'S' and 'T'.
  - The optional data will make each row longer than it needs to be. This will have the effect of:
    - taking more space in the database
    - slowing queries
    - potential for data 'corruption' as developers write routines to capture data which is not required due to a misunderstanding of the table structures, e.g. populating surname and company-name with the same value 'just to be sure'.
- Resolution
  - If the above effects are likely to cause problems in the application, it is best to split the mandatory data into one or more separate tables with the same key as the 'master entity'. Any programs which need this data can create or amend the optional table.
  - Sometimes an indicator (or surrogate-key – see later) is added to the master table to indicate the presence of an optional table row in the optional table. In most cases, this is a piece of duplication since the presence of optional data is already indicated by a value in the master-table (e.g. customer-type).
  - Finally, if the optional data is small (or the size of the database is immaterial) then it makes no sense in splitting this data to a separate table.

3 Some of the primary-key columns can be null:
- Identifying the problem
  - One of the main causes of this is where the logical model has 'exclusive arcs', i.e. the key of the table can be from one of a set of 'master entities'.
  - For example, a set of discounts could be applied to a customer, to an order or to an order-line – one, some or all depending on order-type. Hence the key could be customer-id, order-number, order-line-number, order-type. This is fine but what if, in the future, you want to be able to have a discount for all customers (e.g. a summer sale) – now we may have customer-id of null. This may cause a big skew in the distribution of the table, i.e. all the null rows at the front.

- Resolution
  - You could create separate tables to store customer discounts, order discounts etc. but if the discounts have relationships to each other (e.g. they are to be applied in combination) then the programmer has to access several tables and accumulate the information via code.
  - One alternative is to create a discount-id as a unique key with customer-id etc. as rows with secondary indexes on them. However, the secondary indexes will also become skewed with null values.
  - Another possibility is to move the mandatory 'known' values to the front of the key (primary or secondary), e.g. the key becomes order-type, customer-id, order-id, order-line-number. This enables a spread of data throughout the table.

4 There are a large number of columns in the primary key:
- Identifying the problem
  - Third Normal Form (TNF) analysis forces data analysts to define a unique key for an entity. Any detailed entities below this entity will inherit its parent's key and add one or more attributes to make it's own key unique (e.g. Invoice Number on Invoice Header, Invoice Number and Line Number on Invoice Detail). However, this method can leave the data model with some very cumbersome keys (e.g. a commission percent for a salesperson may have their sales-id, product-code, customer-type, region-code, tax-year, sales-discounted-indicator as the key!).
  - Sometimes the unique key to a table is not obvious and hence an analyst has to invent one (e.g. a posting to an account may not be unique by account-code, posting type or date hence an extra, artificial key is added – sequence-number).
  - If a table has more than three columns in its key it is 'suspect'. If it has more than five, it is unworkable.
  - Some of the side-effects of this kind of data structure are:
    - takes a long time to code the SELECT statements for this type of record
    - because of the length of the key, developers can easily miss out a column in a join which will return bad results
    - the DBMS has to reserve more space for the key – this takes more space and also time as the DBMS has to retrieve more from the index pages.
- Resolution
  - One possible method of shortening the length of a key is to split the key (and hence the entity) into two, i.e. have a header and detail table.
    - This can be done by introducing a surrogate key on the header which substitutes for the header part of the key on the detail entity.
    - For example, from our commission table above we could have a header-key of sales-id, product-code, customer-type with a new data item on this table: sales-alt-key-id – this is just a unique number. Then the detail-key is sales-alt-key-id, region-code, tax-year, sales-discount-indicator.
    - Naturally the above process could be done more than once if it was felt necessary.
  - In some instances, the key has become so long in an attempt to make the primary key unique. However, it should be asked whether this table needs a unique key at all.

- Typically, transaction-history tables are only inserted into or selected from. If they are never updated, there is no need to have a unique key.
- Hence the table can be declared with no unique key or, alternatively, declared as 'heap' and only has non-unique secondary indexes to enable faster selection of groups of records.
- Not only does this speed up insertion into the table but it avoids the need to add a column to make the row artificially unique.

5   Columns used for range searches are part of the key:
- Identifying the problem
  - Dates are often used in keys and this can cause some performance problems since:
    - They are often stored in large data types which makes primary key storage large.
    - They are used in a range search, i.e. within this range, e.g. 'date must be before Y and after X' or 'get the latest date' – these kinds of search mean that the DBMS may not use the index and hence the whole table is searched for rows matching the criteria – this is slow.
- Resolution
  - One solution might be to replace the date(s) in the key as a sequence number. These sequence numbers are stored in a header record which specifies last, current, next row (as required). These sequence numbers have to be maintained by programming means but at least they prevent an awful lot of date manipulation.
  - Another solution is to separate the current row from past or future rows by placing them in separate tables. Again a program will be required to shuffle the contents of each table, i.e. to move current rows to history and future rows to current.
  - If the above solutions are inadequate and dates are really required as keys then the use of the surrogate key (as in the earlier problem) could be used. In other words, split the table into header and detail rows with a surrogate key being a foreign key on the header to point to the detail rows. This has the following advantages:
    - it is likely to fool the query-optimizer to access the header first and then get a subset of rows from the detail row
    - hopefully, with a smaller key to handle and a smaller number of rows (in the subset), the DBMS will do the range search faster.

6   Sets of entities which are mandatory in the model but not in real life:
- Identifying the problem
  - The model may indicate (via the ERD diagram) that certain table rows are created together when, in fact, the data may be incomplete (this is indicated by a mandatory relationship).
  - For example, customer, customer order and payment details – can a customer be created without an order? Can an order be created without payment details? In the real world, incomplete or partial information may need to be captured.
  - Questions should be asked of each mandatory relationship on the ERD – will the data always be present in all circumstances? Is it required to capture partial information and return to complete it later?

- Solution
    - To cater for this, some kind of 'incomplete' status needs to be marked on the row to indicate that this data is not to be used in further processing until it has been completed.

Definitions/techniques

Soundex – a method of reducing a string (surname, say) to a standard shortened version so that searching is made on a direct match, e.g. Smith, Smithe, Smyth, Smythe all get shortened to SMTH for searching purposes.

Next steps

See also checklist 6.2 'Database physicalization – five areas of useful tips and tricks'.

6.2 Database physicalization – five areas of useful tips and tricks

Type: Analysis

Checklist description

Database physicalization is a tricky business. There are many dependencies including:

- the particular DBMS query-optimization techniques. Note that these can change per release
- the application usage of the data
- the growth in the data over time and how recently the query statistics have been updated.

The following is a set of techniques that can be used to enhance performance or to revisit a database where performance is beginning to degrade.

Checklist

Tables

- Split tables to get better performance
  - The fewer rows in a table means the DBMS has to use fewer page accesses to get the required data.
  - The fewer columns in a row can improve performance since the DBMS can get more rows in a single page read.
  - Tables can be split vertically (i.e. split out columns) based on:
    - mandatory vs optional data (see checklist 6.1 'What logical data models get wrong (and have to be put right)')
    - dynamic vs static data
    - function – e.g. split out operational data from MIS data.
  - Tables can be split horizontally (i.e. split out rows) based on:
    - subtypes of data, e.g. customers vs prospects
    - current vs historic.
- Merge the tables to get better performance
  - The fewer tables to join means the DBMS has to do fewer page accesses to get the required data.
  - Tables can be merged where there is a one-to-one relationship between the tables and the data from the tables are often accessed together.
- Keep all interface or conversion data in separate tables – do not merge with the 'live' data
  - Interfaces can change over time and it is best to isolate your application from these changes. For example, if you maintain departmental-codes separately from the Finance system, don't store departmental-code in the account-code structure – store it in a lookup so that if the departmental system changes its coding structure you only have one interface table to change.

Primary keys and secondary indices

- Make all keys integer rather than characters as far as possible (even lookups) since these are fastest for database matching in joins etc.

- Typically the most unique parts of the key should be first in sequence in the key declaration, e.g. customer-number comes before customer-type in the key sequence.
  - This rule can be broken where parts of the key may be null.
- Small, static tables may not need a key. If the total size of the values stored is less than 2Kb (a data page) then leave it as heap. The DBMS will read it in one hit anyway without needing a key.
  - Don't put 'wide' columns used for wildcard or range searches in a secondary index – many DBMS will ignore the secondary key and trawl the main table. For example, text searches may not go any faster if the text is in the secondary index. Try creating a soundex field and indexing on that instead, i.e. direct match not a range search.
- Use the query access paths (from analysis) to determine if you need secondary indices on the second part of a compound key or on a foreign key. If the access path is always from this entity to the other foreign entities then a secondary index is not required.
- Avoid having more than three secondary indices on a table – especially if it is a volatile table with many inserts, updates and deletes. The DBMS will struggle to maintain the indices.

Codes and lookups

- Have a generic lookup table for most code/decode values of structure: code-type [integer], code-value [integer], code-short-display [char(3 or 4)], code-description [char(60)], code-display-sequence-number [integer].
- Don't use structured codes. Split out each component as a column in its own right.
- Do not use explicit ranges in codes to denote some special significance (e.g. part nos 1–4000 are made, 4001–9000 are bought. A problem occurs when you start making your 4001 part).

Useful patterns

- If you have a 'wide' table (lots of columns) which may get wider, e.g. storing various characteristics about a customer, use a 'long' table instead with a key: main-key-id (e.g. customer id), characteristic-type [integer], characteristic-value [char(60)].
  - If the data type of the characteristic is significant, e.g. integer, money etc. then declare a conversion table that a simple program can be used to return the correct data-type, e.g. a table with pairs of values – characteristic-type, characteristic-data-type.
- If you have some optional keys – e.g. customer-id or prospect-id – this can be slimmed down to the following columns main-id, main-id-type [integer]. This avoids having nulls in keys.
- In a financial-transaction system where a single transaction may update several balances then place all the balances in a single table with a balance-type on it. In a control table, it is simple to maintain a cross-reference to how each transaction-type affects each balance-type (if at all). This control table can then be used to generate a rule to update the appropriate balances every time a transaction is inserted into the transaction table.

Sundry tips

- Include date/time stamp on insert/update (but not as a trigger otherwise rule loops will occur) – can be used for soft-locking, test-tracing, restart/recovery checking.
- Use VIEWs and UNIONs to embody common but complex join logic. Hence this can be used by many developers, e.g. joining customer and address via an occupancy table would be a good candidate for a VIEW.

- When loading a significant amount of data into a table (e.g. conversion, bank tape etc.), it is better to load into a HEAP table and re-index it afterwards. This will avoid the DBMS trying to restructure the index for each new row added. Also ensure that the table statistics are updated if this is a frequently accessed table.
- It is often better to 'logically delete' a row rather than 'physically delete' it. In this manner, only topmost entities need to be marked rather than detail entities, e.g. Order-Header can be marked as deleted without needing to mark Order-Line.
    - This method keeps the database consistent without having to track down every compound-key and foreign-key of the main entity and make changes.
    - An archive program should be written at some point that does physically delete old data (or at least move it to non-operational copies of tables).
- Ensure that the table statistics for frequently accessed tables are updated on a regular basis (set by the number of inserts or index/key-column updates there have been).

Definitions/techniques

Soundex – a method of reducing a string (surname, say) to a standard shortened version so that searching is made on a direct match, e.g. Smith, Smithe, Smyth, Smythe all get shortened to SMTH for searching purposes.

Compound-keys – where two significant tables are related, the table that maintains the relationship normally has a primary key that comprises of the main keys from the significant tables, e.g. CustomerOrder may have the key: customer-id, order-id.

Next steps

See also checklist 6.1 'What logical data models get wrong (and have to be put right)'.

6.3 Seventeen quality checks for a physical data model

Type: QA

Checklist description

During the physicalization process of a data model, a Physical Data Design specification should be produced (see checklist 'Moving to a physical data model').

This checklist can be used to check the contents of such a document for completeness.

Checklist

- Physical model reflects business view of data.
- Data is normalized and only physicalized on exception.
- There is consistent data naming.
- Integrity rules have been specified.
- Nulls and defaults have been specified.
- It contains the expected volume of rows per (key) table.
- It contains the expected volume of query hits.
- It identifies the growth expected per day, week, month, year.
- It identifies the top ten access paths including main data used as 'key'.
- It identifies the top ten 'hit' entities per insert, update, delete, read.
- Its indexes are based on volumes and access paths.
- Its indexes are of correct structure.
- The fill factors are sufficient.
- Optimization per entity is identified and cross-referenced to control program.
- Data archiving functions are identified (and consistent with relationship tree).
- Peaks of data usage is identified – volume, frequency, occurrence.
- The data backup strategy is specified and cross-referenced to control program.

Definitions/techniques

Optimization – the process of resetting the DBMS statistics about a table that the DBMS uses to construct query paths to the data. If these statistics are not updated periodically, the DBMS may choose inappropriate methods to get to the data thus slowing down system performance.

Next steps

The physicalized database structures can now be used by developers for system building.

6.4 What modules to add into every application build

Type: Analysis

Checklist description

Often systems design considers only the functions that are immediately apparent to the business user. However, there are many elements that should be built into the system as a matter of course in order that the system is of production-build quality.

Quality systems are reliable (error free), complete (suitable, rounded functionality), easy to maintain, flexible, efficient (do the job quickly or simply), effective (do the right job).

To achieve this, some analysis is required to determine all the components that are required to be built and how they are to be used – a systems infrastructure.

Use this checklist to check what components need to be built into the system from day 1.

Checklist

Common modules

Common modules can form the backbone of a system – the cradle, if you like, into which all the business functionality is held. Often, once developed, common modules can be reused in further, unrelated systems.

In a good systems architecture, the following common modules should be developed and used throughout the development:

- Access control and security
  - How do individuals gain access to the system? What verification process do they go through?
  - What individuals are allowed to do once they have passed the verification process (function access and authorization limits)?
  - What individuals are allowed to see once they have passed the verification process (data access)?
- Data validations – see checklist 6.7 'What to include in a common error detection and handling'.
- Error handling – see checklist 6.7 'What to include in a common error detection and handling'.
- Report printing and distribution.
- Common calculations
  - Income, interest, benefit and profit calculation routines used by both on-line and batch.
  - Multi-currency input/output conversion.
- Operations on a complex or critical data table.
- Date manipulation
  - 'Working day' calculation and return nearest working date – forwards or backwards?
  - Ascertain whether date difference of same day should give result of 1 or 0.
  - Use an internal date setting rather than the system date – this will make it easier to test and avoids any processing issues when the process crosses midnight.

- Activity log
  - Collection of performance statistics and security information:
    - which functions used when and by whom? You can use this for security and to determine if a feature is in use or needs further training etc.
    - failed access attempts.
  - Maintain backup log (plus use of check digits on critical values).
  - Collect DEBUG and diagnostic information (with an on/off parameter):
    - conditional path identification
    - critical data access, statement, procedure, loop id (i.e. give a unique number to each critical point and action in the program)
    - table accesses and number of rows returned
    - number of times through a loop, i.e. a counter.

Locking strategy

There is always a danger in multi-user systems that two users want to update the same piece of data at the same time. This can cause problems. If two users try to update a customer's address, say, which address is the correct one?

To avoid these problems, a locking strategy must be adopted that locks the data being updated by one user from simultaneous updates requested by another user. The following are some of the approaches to locking that could be used:

- Optimistic locking strategies
  - This strategy is based on the assumption that contention between users for the same piece of data is small. Hence the system is optimistic that contention will not occur.
  - Many business applications have been built with non-optimistic locking solutions. However, these are overkill since the chance of two or more users wanting to update the same piece of data at the same time is extremely remote in most business applications.
  - Optimistic locking solutions are generally loose and cheap. Most of them leave any locking resolution up to the DBMS or operating system rather than impose a locking solution within the application itself.
  - Note that some DBMS and OpSys locking strategies lock pages of data (2K blocks) rather than individual rows of data.
- Pessimistic locking strategies
  - This strategy is based on the assumption that there will be some contention of updates between users. The pessimistic view implies that some formal mechanism should exist to resolve conflicts (rather than leave it to the DBMS or OpSys to decide).
  - There are two basic ways of enforcing locking – hard and soft. 'Hard locking' is where the data is locked by the DBMS or OpSys based on a request by the application to do so. Soft locking is where the application manages the locking entirely by application logic.
  - Note that even if soft locking is the approach adopted, some hard locking is always invoked by the DBMS or OpSys for its own locking purposes.
  - Some soft locking mechanisms might be:
    - time stamps rows when retrieved and only allows update if the time stamps match
    - check-in of primary-key of row on retrieval into a 'row-locked' table and delete when row updated. Every attempt to access a row always checks the 'row-locked' table before the row is allowed to be retrieved

- setting of a flag on the row on retrieve to indicate row is locked. This is then cleared on update
- set the system to single user for heavy processes, e.g. overnight batch run – effectively locks the whole database by disabling any kind of on-line user login.

Maintenance Facilities

Alongside the modules that carry out or support the business transactions, there needs to be a set of maintenance functions that keeps the system running smoothly either by inserting data to be used or clearing away the rubbish.

Here is a sample of functions that may need to be added:

- Code table maintenance
  - Screen-based applications typically contain fixed lists of values in, say, drop-down boxes. These values are normally stored as codes with suitable decodes (English descriptions).
  - One single code/decode table can be built to contain all these codes and hence a single maintenance routine can be written to maintain it.
  - This table could possibly contain:
    - code-group – indicates the grouping of codes
    - code-type – the individual separate value within a group
    - code-description – the description often used as the value shown on the screen
    - code-sequence – the display sequence of codes for the drop-down box placing more common values higher in the sequence
    - code-default-indicator – indicates that this code is the default
    - code-valid-indicator – indicates if this is a valid code or a 'dummy' header for this group (e.g. 'Please select a value' might be a default, dummy entry in this group with sequence = 1 which is used to populate the dropdown on screen).
- Build in backups and recovery points
  - Although system crashes are unwelcome they should not be unexpected. Developers need to take a careful look at this aspect of the application module design.
  - There are a number of backup mechanisms that could be employed:
    - database checkpoints or savepoints
    - disk copies and images
    - tape dumps
    - transaction logging.
  - The purpose of placing deliberate recovery points is to minimize disruption to the business in the event of a crash. This can be done by placing system backups at points where it is easy to recover to.
  - These backup points could be placed:
    - before/after heavy processing (e.g. before/after overnight batch)
    - during expected 'low volume' periods, e.g. lunchtime
    - prior to the updating of an external system
    - prior to the updating from an external system
  - Backups may need to include:
    - database
    - import/export data and/or files
    - temporary tables
    - system environment variables and system files (e.g. registry settings, .ini files etc.)

- Data archive provision
  - As databases get more densely populated, performance can degrade as DBMS have to access more index information to find the data being requested. Hence there may need to be archive facilities to keep the database 'clean'.
  - There are different types of archiving function (a mixture can be used in the same application as desired):
    - Copy data to a database mirror and remove from the master.
    - Remove data to a special archive table (normally reducing what is stored, e.g. summary records are created from detailed transaction records).
    - Take a table dump to a flat file and then onto tape and delete required rows.
  - Key factor to establish what is the timescale of interest in the data?
  - One particular factor that influences the design of archiving is the cascade-delete problem:
    - If you remove certain rows, what happens to other rows that contain primary and foreign-key pointers to the removed rows?
    - If you also remove these 'foreign-key' rows with foreign-keys, what happens to the rows that point to the foreign-key rows?
    - There needs to be careful assessment of what can be archived and what cannot.

Other module considerations

Here are a few areas that might need to be planned across all modules:

- What are the common screen handling characteristics? – see checklist 6.12 'Four standards to apply to the user interface'.
- Is multi-currency or multi-lingual processing expected or required?
- Should there be some 'manual override' facilities to change certain critical fields in case of emergency?

Definitions/techniques

None.

Next steps

See checklist 6.5 'Individual module quality – key questions to ask' to see how these items will affect actual module build.

6.5   Individual module quality – key questions to ask

Type: QA

Checklist description

The quality of an individual module is difficult to measure. All quality measures are subjective and sometimes quality rules have to be broken for the greater good. However, it is desirable to attempt to have some kind of consistency of approach across modules and this checklist can be used as a 'yardstick' to measure some aspects of module quality.

It might be best applied in a desk-checking or walkthrough setting. It is recommended that the critical modules are put through this kind of QA testing since these pieces of code will be subject to the most stress and possibly the most change.

Checklist

General

- Has a defensive programming approach been taken?
    - It test all inputs for validity (even if already done so in calling module).
    - Where a mathematical division occurs in the code, is there a pre-divide test for zero divide (this will crash many processors)?
    - Use of drop before creation of (temporary) tables.
- Has the naming convention been adopted in all places?
    - Is there sensible naming even when the naming convention does not apply, e.g. use module specific temp table names rather than TEMP1, say?
- Has the locking strategy been adopted?
- Will transaction integrity be maintained?
    - Have start/end transaction points been identified?
    - Will all or no updates occur or are there many 'linked' transactions (all or nothing update – no partial – can be done in parts by 'soft integrity')?
    - Has rollback been specified in case of error?
    - What should happen to the program or system after rollback has occurred?
- Does the module leave appropriate 'fingerprints'?
    - Sets a table-column date/time stamp for insert/update operations (can be used as soft-locking mechanism).
    - Invokes the security and activity logging module.

Complexity

- How complex is the module construction?
    - Is it easy to follow?
    - Can someone else maintain it? (Only if this is a genuine need and not a throwaway program.)
    - How big is the module?
        - Does it provide many functions (e.g. complex calculator) or one simple one?
        - Sometimes big is beautiful (all functions in one place) and small is ugly (too many components to keep track of).
        - Rule should be whether the module can be reused as it is.

- Is it well commented?
  - Should be present in all code.
  - Better to explain a block of code with a block of comment rather than line-by-line comments.
  - There should be a module version no as declared as a constant as well as a commented version history.
- How easy is it for module to be changed?

Links to other modules
- How many interface calls to other modules?
- Does it use all the common modules required?
  - Error handling.
  - Debug information collation.
  - Activity and security logging.
  - Common calculations (e.g. date manipulation).
  - Security validation (especially required if application is intended for the Internet).

Testable
- Can it be tested?
  - Is there a test harness and a realistic set of replayable test cases (that can be enhanced and augmented)?
  - Has a volume test been conducted to check for bottlenecks early on in the process?
- Can it be shown to embody the functionality required by the Design Specification – no more and no less?
- Use of date parameter rather than system date – this will allow:
  - batch routines to span midnight without adverse effects
  - testing cycles to be run independent of the machine date (e.g. speed up monthly cycle testing, test for Feb. 29th etc.)

Definitions/techniques

None.

Next steps

See checklist 6.6 'Transactions and how to design them'. See also checklist 6.4 'What modules to add into every application build'.

6.6 Transactions and how to design them

Type: QA

Checklist description

Most business systems are made up of transactions. A transaction, in this context, is one or more updates to a file or table such that the end state of the data reflects the business need.

It is important to ensure that each transaction (insert, update, delete) is complete and not lacking anything. There are various attributes of each transaction which need to pass what is called the ACID test (see checklist below). The purpose of the test is to ensure each transaction is isolated and independent so that there are clear recovery points. This means that should anything go wrong in the middle of a transaction, you can go back to a safe point, i.e. returning the system and database to a consistent state.

This checklist contains the key tests to apply to transactions. Whilst it may not be possible to check every transaction in the system, the crucial update transactions should have the following attributes:

Checklist

Atomic
- Inspect where there is a set of complex actions to perform or the database is complex.
- Test that the transaction will either succeed completely or fail completely – no partial updates.
- Test that the transaction leaves the database in a consistent state not waiting for another transaction to 'finish the job'.

Consistent
- Inspect where there are inserts or updates on a number of tables or files in a single transaction.
- There are various types of transaction which should be checked:
  - header and detail lines are written as a consistent set – invoices, orders etc.
  - insertion of rows updates a total – journal posting, cash batch entry
  - entities and link entities where the entity is not optional in the relationship.

Isolation
- Inspect where there are multiple transactions affecting the same entity as it goes through its lifecycle.
- Test that each transaction does not interfere with the operation of the others. Nor should it depend on the assumption that the others have been run or not run (i.e. it should check all its starting conditions as part of its own process).

Durable
- Inspect where there might be some delay between committing the transaction and its data being available to other processes.
- Once a transaction has completed, its actions should be immediately present for other transactions to perceive.

- Problems can occur in the following areas:
  - where data is stored in memory for use by other programs
  - where data is stored in memory before writing to disk (e.g. caching)
  - where data is stored locally before being 'centralized'
  - where there is database replication (one-way or two-way)
  - where DBMS locking is at page level rather than row level.
- There are various techniques available to solve some of these problems:
  - locking data until it is committed
  - implementing a time stamp checking and locking strategy
  - explicitly forcing a memory 'flush' to disk at transaction end
  - implementing a 'two-phase' commit strategy
  - implementing a 'collision' reporting strategy.
- Some of these solutions require more work than others. When choosing a solution, bear in mind:
  - how likely is a collision on that data?
  - can updates be queued and will performance suffer unduly?
- The basic strategy should be to lock late and release as early as possible.

Other
- There shouldn't be any calls to other modules within a transaction.
- A transaction should always have a clear beginning and end.

Definitions/techniques

Page-level locking – this occurs where the DBMS locks a block of data (say a 2K block) rather than an individual row. Depending on row width, a page can contain several rows. Hence for the duration of the update, updates to other rows on the page are queued. This can cause a bottleneck for high-hit rows, e.g. next-number allocation columns.

Next steps

Any key transaction which does not fulfil these criteria should be recoded to the criteria.

Most transaction-based systems also declare 'start transaction', 'end transaction' markers so that developers, when detecting an error, can ROLLBACK to the start of the transaction. Depending on the type of error, they may retry the transaction or abort (normally passing the error back to a user).

See also the checklist 6.7 'What to include in a common error detection and handling'.

6.7   What to include in common error detection and handling

Type: QA

Checklist description

Most if not all systems need to have an error detection capability. There are two possible approaches:

(a) Leave the handling of errors to each individual developer to detect, report and navigate.
(b) Produce common routine(s) for each developer to use.

Approach (a) generally gives less than satisfactory degree of cover since:

* inexperienced or lazy developers don't include all kinds of error trapping in their code thus exposing the application to potential crashes
* experienced, hard-working developers sometimes forget things and therefore some error trapping doesn't get coded.

Naturally, someone could argue that approach (b) could suffer from the same problems. True, but at least with common routines, the list of errors being trapped can increase in one place (rather than across all the different programs in a system). Hence it builds into a repository of errors. A fix-once rather than fix-many must be a cheaper and more resilient approach.

This checklist can be used to define what should be included (in the first instance) in a common error routine.

Checklist

1   Test for errors after each transaction or table operation. Tests to include:
* deadlock detected
* number of row(s) written, updated, deleted per table or file operation
    * Can it be more than one?
    * Can it be zero?
* The row has been locked and stayed locked during this transaction, i.e. locked from the moment the data was read and, perhaps, displayed on screen for update until committed back to the database. (This can be done through the effective use of time stamps if it is not built into the DBMS.)

2   Employ fault-detection techniques
* Timing checks:
    * allow function calls to time out – may be looping or some other problem (lost connection or session)
    * in client server – how does the client know when the server is not responding and what does it do?
    * in client server – how does the server know if the client is still there and what does it do (session management)?
    * how many database retries are allowed? What if the connection fails?
    * for communications-based software, what if the phone line is interrupted? How do you detect this?

- Tolerance checks:
  - use a rough calculation on inputs with standard deviations to check output value. If the real calculated value varies significantly then flag a warning.
- Parity check:
  - useful for string manipulation or streams of data – e.g. row + column counts, checkdigit, word count.
- Integrity checks:
  - ensure data relationships are maintained. No orphans or lone parents.
- Domain checks:
  - values within their domain, e.g. dates, post codes, amounts
  - fields should have common validation procedures to ensure consistent storage and handling.
- Diagnostic check:
  - take a set of known inputs and outputs and run them through the system.

3   Error messages must not be:

- too abrupt or rude and use swear words
- condescending
- vague – not enough information, e.g. 'An error has occurred'
- unhelpful – no clues as to which program or where in the program, the error has occurred.

4   Error handling:

- Aborts transaction and performs rollback (see checklist 6.6 'Transactions and how to design them').
- Places user back on appropriate screen and field.
- Flags error to batch manager so that no other jobs in the batch are commenced.
- Return value is set with success or failure after each transaction.

Definitions/techniques

None.

Next steps

See also checklists 6.6 'Transactions and how to design them' and 6.5 'Individual module quality – key questions to ask'.

6.8 How to distribute modules to servers

Type: To do

Checklist description

Once a logical design has been through its initial phases of physical design, the splitting of functions into deliverable programs and components is the next stage of physical design. To determine how best to distribute those programs and components across the physical hardware architecture, use this checklist.

Checklist

Initial distribution
● Place programs and components based on their type:
  – user service components (screens etc.) on the PC or Web server
  – data service components (SQL calls etc.) on the data server
  – business transaction components on a business server (often synonymous with the data server).

Apply performance constraints
● Review the initial distribution for potential bottlenecks. Look at each component and the server on which it is sited:
  – Has the server sufficient capacity to handle requests for its component?
  – How much inter-component communication is there and how, by moving components, can this be minimized?
  – Are there component dependencies (e.g. sequences) that would be affected if there was a failure in a server or network? Can the risk of failure be minimized by changing the distribution of the components?

Possible considerations
● Move components that are always called together to the same server.
● Move components closest to the resource(s) they use most heavily or where the network traffic is likely to be high.
● Utilize pooling techniques or 'early binding' techniques to reduce CPU load.

Definition/techniques

Pooling – rather than have to create connections or services on the fly, create a pool of ones that are ready to be used (already in memory). These can be allocated when a genuine call comes in (i.e. pool management).

Early binding – start all the processes and connections required at application start rather than waiting for them to be called. This also applies to query paths within a database which can be set up in advance rather than calculated by the DBMS at query execution time.

Next steps

As can be seen from above, the distribution of software to servers is a 'suck-it-and-see' approach with a few guidelines. However, by iteratively testing the configuration, it should be possible to come up with a suitably performing application. If not, there may be some fundamental performance issues that are resident in the design which cannot be fixed by server configuration — see checklist 6.9 'Finding the big four performance bottlenecks'.

Finally, it should be noted that as the application becomes more widely used, the configuration should be revisited. Over time, an application is likely to have:

- more concurrent users = more sessions and database connections
- more transactions = more data moving across a network and a busier data server with potentially more page locks
- more data residing on databases = more data retrieved in queries and hence more data moving across a network.

Consequently, it's important to review performance and configuration in the light of these changes.

6.9 Finding the big four performance bottlenecks

Type: Analysis

Checklist description

At some point in the life of most applications, performance problems become evident. It can be during development and testing or, even worse, later during live usage.

Sometimes a performance bottleneck can be predicted. This provides a place to start work. Often, however, a bottleneck appears from 'out of the blue' and further analysis is required.

This checklist is intended to assist in determining performance bottlenecks and give some hints on how to overcome them.

Checklist

Query design
- Run query traces on all SQL calls and ensure that there is not a many-to-many retrieve (also known as a Cartesian product). This is normally caused by a bad join.
- Check the creation and destruction of temporary tables. This can slow up the DBMS since it also updates its table-inventory lists.
  - This can be solved by retrieving the data into an array (rather than a temporary table) and processing it in memory (rather than on disk).
- Use integers as key columns for joining tables rather than character columns – the DBMS can match integers faster than characters (which require it to do a slow character-by-character compare).
  - Using integer lookup codes rather than character codes is a key performance enhancing trick.
- Check all SQL joins that all tables are needed in the join. Often there is some redundancy.
  - Only use tables where they have a column being retrieved or they are a link table, e.g. take a common scenario of three tables: customer, occupancy, address where a customer can be an occupant in more than one address (over time). Similarly an address can have more than one customer occupant. Occupancy has a key of customer_id and address_id. Hence, given a customer_id, to find their address we only need to join occupancy and address. We do not need to include the customer table in the join (since we already have the customer_id).

Table design
- Is one table being 'hit' a lot (e.g. a next-number allocation table)?
  - Possibly split the table.
  - Increase the fill factor to lower the page lockouts or waits.
- In a complex process, does the table design 'fight' the process design?
  - For example, if a table has to be joined many times to itself to achieve a requirement then maybe the table design is flawed.
  - Typically, some tables may need to be denormalized by carrying calculated columns rather than have a process calculate the value every time it is needed.

- Are there columns in a table which are historic and hence ignored (e.g. old address records)?
  - Leaving historic data in a 'live' table can have a number of performance implications:
    - database has to retrieve more pages to find the data that you want (since it is spread out amongst the historic data)
    - programs have to include logic to navigate around historic data (especially if it is date-driven). This makes the programs larger than required.
  - Where possible, store historic data in separate tables (or even separate databases) as soon as it becomes historic.
    - If it is used to calculate some value, calculate the value and store it as you are removing the historic data. Subsequently all programs use the calculated value rather than the historic data.

Memory

- Does the program require large amounts of memory? Is it storing too much in variables or arrays?
  - As a system runs out of memory, it starts 'paging' (writing memory to disk) to pick up when it needs it. This will slow the application down a considerable degree.
  - If data is being stored in memory out of habit for some future but unspecified purpose, then the program should be written to only capture and store data for its current need.
  - Also, a program should release memory as soon as it no longer needs it even if it may be needed in the near future.
- Does the program have a large memory 'footprint'?
  - If the program runs on a shared processor or if a user can start many 'memory-hungry' programs on the same server then memory can easily run out.
    - One solution may be to write the program to become multi-threaded, i.e. the same code is used but each user keeps a data area that is unique to them and pointers to where they are in the program. The right choice of programming environment (languages, tools and compilers) can assist in the development of this type of code.
    - Similarly, the use of pooled resources (e.g. database connections) can reduce the memory overhead. In this case there is a 'resource pool manager' who allocates a resource it is holding ready. When the 'user' (i.e. the program) finishes with the resource, it gives it back to the resource pool manager who keeps it available for the next user. These types of resource-pools are often faster and more memory efficient than each program managing its own resources.
  - Is the program too large, i.e. 'bloatware'?
    - Can the program be split into smaller, lightweight programs that can call each other if necessary?
    - Apply the 80:20 rule to program design since the majority of the functionality may reside in 20 per cent of the program – the other 80 per cent is to provide additional, rarely used functions or facilities.
  - Note that it may be worth investing in additional memory management to ensure that released memory really does become available to the operating system. A number of well-known programs suffer from 'memory leakage', that is, although they release memory, the operating system still considers it 'locked'. Over time, the operating system runs out of memory even though no application is running.

Program design

- Does the program contain complex logic?
  - Is an algorithm broken down into its logically constituent parts or does it try to achieve too much in one go?
    - Some loops in algorithms are always invoked whether they are required or not. This causes the program to execute for longer than necessary. By breaking the algorithm down into appropriate portions these loops become more visible and can be by-passed when optimal.
    - Sometimes even when a stopping condition is reached, most programs continue to iterate to the end of the loop counter. This should be detected and resolved.
  - Does the program deal with one case at a time when it could deal with many at a time?
    - Quite often in relational DB systems, all the cases that require a particular treatment (e.g. interest calculation) are picked up and then each case is handled one at a time (in a loop). In most cases, using SQL, the whole group can be handled together, i.e. apply successive updates to all rows until the solution is reached.
  - Alternatively, it could be how software is deployed across the different hardware platforms (see checklist 6.8 'How to distribute modules to servers').

Definitions/techniques

There are several definitions/techniques in this section which deserve much fuller treatment than can be afforded here. If you wish to find out more, I suggest you investigate using the Internet or find suitable training courses.

Next steps

A large number of performance problems can be solved by revisiting the design and looking for the above opportunities. But don't forget, sometimes the cheapest and easiest fix is to throw hardware at the problem:

- more memory or disks
- faster processor
- more processors
- expand bandwidth.

6.10 Why projects don't achieve software reuse

Type: To do

Checklist description

Despite the widespread use of object orientated techniques, there is still too little software reuse. So if object orientation doesn't deliver software reuse, what will?

The answer, of course, isn't object orientation *per se*. In fact, software reuse can be achieved without object orientation at all (although the technique is a good facilitator of reuse). The answer lies in the desire for reuse and the control processes applied to the development process.

This checklist is intended to provide a road-map to achieving reuse.

Checklist

1   Develop a corporate architecture:
    (a) Map all uses of customer information and other business-centric data.
    (b) Where do you expect reuse to occur?
    (c) Look at the information flow across boundaries of the organization – what do people share?
    (d) Reuse works better with business concepts than low-level, technical objects and modules.

2   Have a librarian to whom all project designs go to for spotting reuse capabilities. Reward this person if they can redeploy an object or module:
    (a) Need to 'seek out and destroy' any 'not invented here' attitudes amongst the developers. Ensure they get some reward each time the module they have written is reused.
    (b) Ensure that, where possible, the original developer gets to enhance their own module when improvements are required. This generates and maintains ownership and professional pride.
    (c) All reused objects and components need to be of high-calibre quality to qualify for reuse. The librarian should have the power to assess the suitability of a module proffered for re-use. By 'quality', this means:
        –   well-documented design
        –   well-structured code
        –   defensive programming style error checking
        –   easy-to-understand published interfaces.

3   Ensure there is proper configuration management as objects and modules improve. The code could even be version threaded.

4   Look for patterns of behaviour across different business systems and create a generic handler of these types of problem. For example:
    •   Bill-of-materials type structures have common behaviour in different applications – the implementation of these is invariably the same:
        (i)   from a parent, find all its children
        (ii) from a child, find parent and ultimate patriarch

  (iii) find all the leaf nodes

  (iv) produce an indented list top-down from a specific point.

(b) Start/end date processing:

  (i) get all the rows which are live as at a certain date

  (ii) when the next record starts, this record should end

  (iii) apply rates which vary over time to balances which vary over time

  (iv) an event has occurred that splits this time-based record into two (either in the past which leads to a recalculation) or the future (in which case it is ignored until it comes into effect).

(c) Providing the data names remain the same throughout the different instances of these patterns, then the same code could be reused (e.g. start_date, end_date, parent_id, child_id etc.)

5 Map functions to business processes not technical objects:

(a) If you create ten thousand technical objects then it will take just as long to find and deploy those objects as to build it from scratch.

(b) You need large business objects not technical ones to achieve reuse.

Definitions/techniques

Version threading – where a module is always passed a parameter of which version that module is to work in. This enables backwards compatibility.

Next steps

See also checklist 6.4 'What modules to add into every application build'.

6.11 How to find the causes of extremely elusive errors

Type: Analysis

Checklist description

Bugs crop up in systems all the time. Probably the amount of time spent trying to find bugs is ten times the amount of time spent developing virgin code. Bugs can show up at any time in any place – during development, during testing and 'out in the wild'.

This is a checklist of the hardest to spot bugs. Use it to produce a 'process of elimination' in tracking down the elusive cause of a bug.

Checklist

- Data type mismatch
    - Integer multiplied by a float may truncate results.
    - Check the field lengths of data columns versus internal variables. This may truncate results.
    - Upper, lower and mixed case mismatch between the names of data variables.
- Non-initialization of internal variables
    - Check the use of nulls. Are they allowed/expected? What do they mean?
    - Are all integer, float, money fields set to zero at the start of the module (even if the manual says you don't have to)?
    - Are variables initialized at all?
    - Are variables used for more than one purpose? Split them.
- Special characters used? (Quotes, brackets, operands)
    - Which type of quote mark is permitted – single or double?
    - Have you used single or double quotes in character matching (e.g. variable = ABC versus variable = 'ABC')?
    - Special meanings of single and double occurrences of a symbol (e.g. '=' versus '= =' meaning 'assignment' versus 'equivalence').
    - Operand symbols in the right order (e.g. j+ + vs + +j).
    - Use of brackets and proper bracket matching especially if there is an 'OR' in the clause.
- Query retrieving no rows
    - Upper, lower and mixed case mismatch between the contents of data variables. This can be hard to spot since people tend to convert these without noticing when comparing two values.
    - Extra spaces in the text (very hard to spot on screen).
    - Unprintable or hidden characters present in the field (need to use a hexidecimal viewer to spot these).
    - Is data being cached and not written to disk hence not available for a subsequent read?
- Fatal errors, crashes, memory address problems
    - Check all mathematical division statements for the divisor being zero (dividing by zero will crash many systems).
    - Check all loops for falling off the start/end of an array. Do arrays start at zero or 1 and what is the end condition testing for?

- Are there any hidden buffer-size limits, file-open limits or rows-retrieved limits (especially if these are defined in header files not actually checked by a developer but included in the executable at compile time)?
- Has the system sufficient free resources?
- Sundry
  - Is a ROLLBACK hiding the error condition so that it cannot be spotted?
  - Is there a 'hidden' rule or trigger being fired on one of the updated tables? Could it be that it is a condition within this trigger failing?
  - Are you comparing/using like with like in terms of the data content?
    - money amounts: one in dollars, one in Euros
    - integer measurements: metric vs imperial
    - integer ages: years vs months.
  - Hard-coded strings which have changed in the environment but not in the code (or vice versa):
    - directories/filenames
    - DB connections.
  - Is the version of the program (and all the programs it calls) in step?
  - Has a licence run out on one of the system-software applications (e.g. OpSys, DBMS, TP monitor etc.)?
  - Have all the system variables (logicals, directories etc.) been set up correctly? Does the user permission of the program allow it to open or use those variables? Are there different user, group and system levels of the same variable? Is the program using the right one?
  - Is a system variable being changed by another program, e.g. is the system-date changing mid-program (i.e. over midnight) causing queries to retrieve different results?
  - Has error checking been applied to all SQL calls (i.e. the error reported may be a consequence of an error not detected earlier)?
    - Also check that the program is using valid inputs (i.e. has another program allowed invalid data to be stored or passed)?
    - A 'defensive programming' approach should be used to validate all inputs.
  - Don't ignore the obvious. Is it a known DBMS or operating system or compiler bug?

Definitions/techniques

Defensive programming – a technique to validate all inputs in every program so that it is isolated from errors in other programs, i.e. all its errors are errors of its own making.

Next steps

See checklist 6.7 'What to include in common error detection and handling'.

6.12 Four standards to apply to the user interface

Type: QA

Checklist description

There are many factors to consider when designing a user interface. As with most IT-related subjects, there are many helpful books to guide the unwary in the process of creating user-friendly screens.

This checklist is a 'memory jogger' of some of the issues to include in screen design. This list can be used to generate a screen design standard for the particular application in hand. It is desirable to have a common standard since:

- it helps with user training and familiarization
- it is easier to test because abnormal behaviour is more easy to detect when there is a standard 'look and feel'.

Checklist

Layout standards
The 'look' standards should cover:

- font and font size per heading level including font settings: bold, italics etc.
- creation of a common screen header for every screen containing, for example:
  - screen name
  - program module identifier and version
  - date/time (for screen-print purposes)
- use of colour in text, in error messages, background
- where pop-ups are positioned
- where error and status messages are displayed
- order of 'yes/no' buttons should be consistent everywhere
- data should be grouped logically
- data labels should be aligned
- data labels for data-entry fields should contain guidance as to the format expected in the field, e.g. 'Start Date (dd-mmm-yyyy):'
- data-entry fields should be aligned
- data-entry fields should indicate whether the field is mandatory
- common function buttons should be in the same place on every screen.

Screen handling standards
The 'feel' standards should cover:

- use of common function controls and switches which have the same effect in all places.
- pop-up screens are used consistently, i.e. this type of field will always have a pop-up, this type of action always results in a pop-up etc.
- formats for data are consistent. Always x characters big, validation is always the same (e.g. date input is always dd-mmm-yyyy etc.)
- tab sequences of fields follow a natural and visually expected pattern, e.g. from left to right, top to bottom or from top to bottom, left to right.

Overall screen routing

- The overall screen routing can be one of several patterns:
  - hub – where each screen is accessed from a 'hub' screen and returns to the 'hub' screen when it is closed
  - hierarchical – where a screen is at the bottom of a hierarchy of menus and sub-menus or processes and sub-processes
  - business thread based – where a screen appears as appropriate within a business thread and links to the next screen in the thread. This could be business-thread and data-input dependent, e.g. next screen is DirectDebit mandate only if payment is required and direct-debit method has been selected by user.
- The screen-routing approach could be selected by balancing:
  - which approach best matches the business process
  - what is the least confusing of the approaches
  - after long-term usage, what is the least annoying approach.

Sundry screen standards

Particular messages and pop-ups to include:

- logon message which states unauthorized access is prohibited
- messages to say system is still running during a long transaction
- use of 'confirm' pop-up before taking critical action
- allow for paper alignment – especially if special stationery, e.g. cheques, pre-printed invoices, headed paper, customer statements etc.

Default values

- Be careful of allowing defaults or drop-down lists especially on values which could be used for dimension analysis in an MIS system. People tend to enter what is easiest, quickest or whatever the system will accept. Hence an analysis by product sold could show 'Other' as 90 per cent since everyone knows the system will accept this value.

Validation

- No code behind buttons. It's harder to find trace – all code should be in functions.

Definitions/techniques

None.

Next steps

See also checklist 6.5 'Individual module quality – key questions to ask'.

7
QA and testing checklists

7.1 Establishing the need for testing and QA

Type: Analysis

Checklist description

Testing is a critical success factor in any IT project. However, it is often added onto the end of a project. As a result, as a project continues, the time window for testing gets squeezed with disastrous consequences.

Quality is not something that can be bolted onto a system afterwards. It has to be part of the process. As testing has to be planned upfront, a business case must be made for this.

The following checklist outlines why building in testing is essential.

Checklist

- IT personnel have a limited amount of time to develop a system but users have an infinite amount of time to break it.
- Users expect quality and are less and less prepared to accept 'shoddy' goods.
- Quality cannot be added to a 'shoddy' system.
- Testing at the end of a system's lifecycle will tend to show expensive to fix faults (e.g. requirements errors, bad system design, bad data model) rather than cheap ones (e.g. screen label typos).
- The quality of the whole system depends on the quality of its parts. The system is only as strong as its weakest link. It is therefore essential to ensure quality at all levels.
- If insufficient time is allowed for testing then:
    - not everything is covered – increasing risk of unknowns
    - testing is rushed at last minute – increasing risk of missing the obvious errors
    - attention to detail is sacrificed – increasing risk of failure
    - people test for success and skip testing for failure – increasing risk of unpredictable results
    - system is implemented and fails – increasing business success risk
    - system is implemented – increasing business operations risk
    - people involved in system development become demoralized – increases risk of critical staff turnover.
- Due to the timescale of systems development, we cannot afford to wait until the end of development before testing of the system starts.

Definitions/techniques

None.

Next steps

Once the need for testing has been established, it is important to set limits on the amount of testing that can actually be achieved – see checklist 7.2 'Setting the scope of testing – avoiding the bottomless pit'.

7.2 Setting the scope of testing – avoiding the bottomless pit

Type: Analysis

Checklist description

Testing, as has often been said, can only prove the presence of errors never the absence of them. A corollary of this maxim is that you can never do too much testing – testing is a bottomless pit. Testing may take up to 40 per cent of the entire project effort.

Business chiefs may balk at that level of spend, so careful analysis of the objectives of testing and the 'cost of not testing' (or cost of system failure) should be prepared. Testing managers must carefully weigh the amount of effort spent in testing. This means understanding, setting and managing the scope of the test effort.

There needs to be a statement of how much testing is to be done, fleshing out what will be covered and what won't be covered.

This checklist identifies five critical areas of an IT system. Beneath each item are samples of different levels of testing that could be adopted. Use the checklist to produce statements of scope to indicate the level of testing required in each of the five areas. The statements could be stated 'as a minimum, the test plan will …' and go on to state 'we expect to test …' ending with 'ideally we will test …'

Checklist

Functionality
- System provides all required business functions.
- System provides critical functions (i.e. transactions that must be there and the business cannot afford to get wrong).
- System provides high usage functions (applying 80:20 principle that 80 per cent of functionality is in 20 per cent of functions).

Data
- System correctly transfers data to/from other systems.
- Database integrity is maintained per transaction even in the case of failure.
- System works as expected after data conversion.

Look and feel
- It is important that the users' impressions of the system are positive as they are the 'customers'.
- System has the agreed screen and report layouts.
- Appropriate error messages are helpful, meaningful, appropriate.

Contingency
- That backup, recovery and restart work.
- That a separate disaster recovery site or machine has been shown to work.

Performance and availability

- System can handle the expected volume at the required performance level.
- System can exceed any expected volumes at better-than-required performance levels.

Definitions/techniques

None.

Next steps

Check your testing scope by considering the worst-case scenario and cost its impact. Is it worth testing for this? How significant is the failure of this item?

Gradually move the boundary back from testing nothing to towards 'test everything' to see where the dividing line is. There is a need to set stop criteria for testing. The results of this investigation should form the Testing Objective documentation – see checklist 7.6 'What test documentation should I maintain for application testing?'.

Once the scope of testing has been determined, the testing should be applied to the project plan and appropriate resources allocated to it – see checklist 7.3 'Ensuring the mix of testing types is present in a project'.

7.3 Ensuring a mix of testing types is present in a project

Type: Analysis

Checklist description

Over the life of a project, testing can be conducted at various levels. It is important to insert the appropriate types of testing at the key points in the project so that overall project quality goals are achieved.

This checklist identifies the two basic types of testing that can occur and at what points in the project should these types of test be employed.

Review the project plans and insert the relevant testing types. These can then be broken down into appropriate tests (see later checklists).

Checklist

Verification testing

Purpose
Basically, poses the question 'Have we built it right?' Each deliverable should be tested to ensure that it has been built according to specification with the applicable standards in place.

Tests to apply
- All documents should have the following initial sections:
  - Document title and document filename (see standards for document filenames).
  - Document set (if part of a suite of documents).
  - Current date, version number, status, latest author.
  - Version history of versions, authors, brief description of changes.
  - Any legal claims or disclaims (e.g. copyright).
  - Contents page.
  - Introductory chapter with the following sections:
    - Background – background of the project
    - Purpose – where this document fits into the project
    - Method – what methods and/or documents have been used or preceded this document. This could include any acknowledgements to individuals who have assisted in the production of the document
    - Scope – what is included and excluded from the boundaries of this document
    - Assumptions – any contexts that are 'taken for granted'
    - Issues – any parts of the document that are incomplete due to unknown or changing requirements (the final version of a document should have the text 'None' in this section).
- The following documents should be QA'd for completeness, internal consistency and conformance to standards as well as consistent any appropriate the 'bigger picture' document.
  - Business Requirements Specification – consistent with Business Process Design document (if any)?
  - System Requirements Specification – consistent with Technical/Architecture/Strategy document (if any)?
  - System Design Specification – will satisfy all stated Business/System Requirements?

- During the build process, as well as conformance to build standards (e.g. commented code, use of standard error routines etc.), the following types of testing should be performed:
  - module or unit testing:
    - does the component work?
    - given the correct inputs, are the correct outputs produced?
    - given the incorrect inputs, are the appropriate errors produced?
  - structural or system testing:
    - do the components work together?
    - are the correct outputs produced which are then correct inputs to the next process?
    - does the system do what it was intended to do?
    - does the system do what it was not intended to do?
  - link or integration testing:
    - does the system provide and accept correct data from other systems?
    - does the system reject incorrect data from other systems?
    - does the system flag and store (for further analysis) data rejected from other systems?
  - volume, capacity, performance or stress testing:
    - does the system manage expected volumes with the performance expected?
    - what volume does the system cease to manage with acceptable performance?

Validate

Purpose

Basically posing the question: 'Have we built the right thing?' We need to test what is required not just what is delivered. Hence there is a strong people-to-project goal emphasis as opposed to an emphasis on software.

Tests to apply

- The following documents should be 'accepted' by the business chiefs:
  - Business Process Description – is the process right? Can it be implemented? Does it compromise any aspect of our business?
  - Business Requirements Specification – will the requirements support the process to the appropriate level? Is anything missing? Is anything superfluous?
  - Service level agreement – are these volumes reasonable? Is the service level overkill or an unreasonable demand?
- The following tests should be applied against the build:
  - functionality:
    - what does the system do?
    - does the system do what it was intended to do?
    - does the system do what it was not intended to do?
  - acceptance:
    - can the system be used as intended by the actual users?
    - does it meet all the stated requirements?
    - does it contain all the functionality they expect?
    - does it accept all the data (and combinations of data) they want to store?
    - does it reject all the data (and all the combinations) of data (including duplicates) that they wish to reject?

- operational:
  - is the system easy to run?
  - are there batch schedules?
  - what is the dependency of batch schedules?
  - batch dependency – jobs and systems that must stop if others fail
  - what happens if the system fails? How do we envisage staff carrying on with their jobs?
  - have we planned and trained for system failure?
  - do we keep planning and training for this? Who is responsible when this happens? See also Chapter 8 'System implementation checklists'.

Definitions/techniques

See the checklists marked as QA throughout the book.

Next steps

Build into the plan the tests appropriate to the deliverables being produced.

Regression testing should not be seen as a different type of testing than the ones above. Regression testing arises when some component(s) of the system fails and needs to be reworked. Hence all the appropriate tests from the list above should be used to retest the component(s) and its integration into the system rather than a special one-off regression test. However, it may be that some additional tests should be added to the test scripts or QA checklists for later use – in order to trap the flaw earlier.

7.4 What to test at two key milestones of a project

Type: QA

Checklist description

Most projects have one testing phase which is when the software is delivered. However, there is another key point where there should be a heavy testing phase and this is when the systems design documentation has been completed.

This checklist can be used to determine what tests should be applied to both key test phases.

Checklist

1   Production of system design documentation:
- As a minimum have the following documents been produced?
    - diagram showing the flow of data from process to process
    - dictionary describing the files, tables and the data (including mandatory/optional, default/nullable values, dependent data values)
    - description of each process
    - diagram showing the relationship between the files and tables
    - layout of the forms, screens and reports.
- Check the minimum documents that:
    - there are enough processes
    - data is accurately described
    - relationships of the files and tables are correct
    - screen and report layouts follow the natural work pattern etc.
- Check each document for:
    - quality – complete, consistent, testable, feasible
    - visibility of the logic
    - understandable and simple
    - open to modification – can expand for future expectations, i.e. not a dead-end solution.

2   Production of application software:
- Major application areas to test:
    - user interface – see screen design testing
    - facility and function – see validation/verification testing
    - sensitivity – what things can change that have an impact on this system (e.g. does the application reside with another application on the same server-box and what happens when the other application runs a batch process?)
    - stress – test till it breaks, then you know the upper limit and can set a measurement device on it
    - volume and performance – keep adding users and transactions until you notice a performance degradation. Try various combinations
    - instability – predictable/unpredictable response times and/or results
    - configuration – is it easy to set up? What can easily be missed that has catastrophic consequences (e.g. batch run date parameter)

- compatibility – does the system rely on particular versions of operating system, drivers and DBMS? What is the upgrade path?
- reliability – mean time between failures
- recover/restart – how fault tolerant is the system? What if there is a power cut? How easy is it to restart?
- archive function exists and causes no data inconsistency
- serviceability – mean time to repair, backup/recover, time to find the fault
- documentation and help screens.
- Major hardware areas to test:
  - CPU usage – multitasking, task mix, optimum task level
  - channel usage – use of peripherals, determine queues, optimize configuration
  - memory usage, i.e. caching level, page 'thrashing'
  - memory leakage
  - disk usage – rotational delay, latency, channel usage, cylinder or head, actuator select, use of buffers, use of packing, use of blocks, amount of free space, use of compression
  - network bandwidth
  - IRQ usage
  - database query optimizers to detect Cartesian-product ($m \times n$ rows) queries – bad joins, bad indexes
  - time to backup
  - time to restore
  - batch-run time (start/end of day, week, month, year)
  - report printing – allows alignment of special stationery, prints and feeds on multipart in bulk.

Definitions/techniques

None.

Next steps

Note that this checklist can be used in combination with the 'Ensuring a mix of testing types is present in a project' checklist (7.3) and also the other detailed checklists throughout this book.

7.5 Setting up the test team – personnel and policies

Type: Analysis

Checklist description

Setting up the test team properly is extremely important to the success of testing. Contrary to the 'boring' view of testing, testing can be proactive, demanding and intellectually challenging. So often the testing activity is given to those who have finished their programming early (a suspect reward mechanism) or given to those in the IT department who aren't being used for anything else.

A better approach would be to involve everyone in testing in some way. Some people may carry more of the work than others but there is no reason why a team of testers cannot be augmented by others for a specific deliverable or test run – if only to let them see what the testers are up against. Another key aspect of allowing everyone to participate in testing is that peer-review is one of the most successful techniques for trapping errors early.

Whoever is conducting tests at particular points through the project lifecycle, the way the test team is set up is important. The following checklist can be used to ensure that the set-up gives the testing effort a fighting chance. It can be used to set up an overall team or when a new team is formed to test some specific deliverable (e.g. a specification walkthrough).

Checklist

1   Test team culture:
   (a)   The team must be empowered.
      (i)   Can the team actually reject anything (i.e. in acceptance testing, can they reject a system as being unacceptable)?
      (ii)   What forces will be brought to bear to dissuade them from exercising this power (if they even have it)?
   (b)   There must be no fear of questioning.
      (i)   Careful of involvement of manager.
      (ii)   Testing must not be linked to reward/punishment systems.
      (iii)   Strong personalities may quench comment.
   (c)   The time allotted must be appropriate to the task in hand.
      (i)   Don't want a 'too-busy-to-get-it-right' atmosphere to prevail.

2   Test team 'modus operandi':
   (a)   A sponsor must be identified who will 'accept' the system once tested.
   (b)   Test-plans must be prepared in advance of software delivery.
   (c)   The sponsor must sign off test plans in advance of testing.
   (d)   Delivery of software to test area must include:
      (i)   authorized incident and change request forms
      (ii)   description of change plus design and requirements specification references (if changed)
      (iii)   listing of program differences between old and new
      (iv)   evidence of unit testing
      (v)   other supporting documents – memos, support-desk documents etc.

(e)   There will be a separation between valid tests (ones it is expected the system will accept) and invalid tests (ones it is expected the system will reject).

(f)   All valid tests will be run before all invalid tests are run.

(g)   Checks will be made to ensure:

    (i)   all changes are as per request form – no more no less

    (ii)   consistency between specifications, change request and actual changes

    (iii)   unit test has tested all branches of changed and new code

    (iv)   use of peer review before change is implemented in case of knock-on effect.

(h)   After testing, sponsor will be shown evidence of testing and asked to authorize release.

(i)   Establish a minimum test data-set, e.g. at least five users, 100 cases etc.

Definitions/techniques

None.

Next steps

As part of planning the testing of a system, it is important to plan how the tests will be recorded – see checklist 7.6 'What test documentation should I maintain for application testing?'

7.6 What test documentation should I maintain for application testing?

Type: To do

Checklist description

If testing is worth doing, it's worth doing well. There are several key test documents that should be maintained:

- in order to prove that adequate testing has been done
- as a basis for sign-off
- to enable testing to be repeated
- to use as a basis for improving the testing culture.

This checklist identifies the testing documents that should be maintained.

Checklist

1   Test objective and scope:
   (a)   Effectively a policy statement to be applied to the specific system being tested which sets the expectation level amongst the testers about what to test and when testing will be deemed complete.
   (b)   It should include objectives so that everyone knows the level of quality expected.
   (c)   The scope of testing should also be set so that everyone knows what is being tested (mandatory), what may be tested (nice to have) and what will not be tested.
   (d)   The level of testing per function can also be stated. Functions may be:
      (i)   tested to destruction (i.e. find its breaking point)
      (ii)   tested to ensure perfect working (i.e. all requirements satisfied or exceeded)
      (iii) tested to ensure satisfactory working (i.e. critical requirements satisfied or exceeded)
      (iv)   tested to ensure working sufficiently (i.e. minimum requirements satisfied)
      (v)   tested for volume.
   (e)   See checklist 7.2 'Setting the scope of testing – avoiding the bottomless pit'.

2   Test thread (also known as test scripts):
   (a)   This identifies an individual line of transactions to achieve a business purpose.
   (b)   It could be a 'cradle-to-grave' process or just the portion of the process within a particular department. It could be a process or sub-process. Examples of individual test threads may be: 'Order Entry' and 'Customer Statement Enquiry'.
   (c)   It should be expressed as a dialogue – what the user types in and how the system should respond, i.e. input and expected output. It is the expected output that is checked and identifies whether the tests have passed or failed.
   (d)   Each action in the thread has a unique step number. The steps can include references to overnight processes so that a single thread can run over several test days. For example:
      (i)   Step 1: Screen 1A – Enter an order with the following details
             Order Name: AAA System

Order Address: Unit 1, Big Industry Estate, Watford, Herts.
Order item: Styrofoam chips Part No: XXX111XXX
Order Quantity: 10 crates

    (ii)   Step 2: Run end-of-day process

    (iii)   Step 3: Screen 4C – Check order present on system

    (iv)   Step 4: Screen 5B – Check customer present on system

    (v)   Step 5: Screen 1B – Approve order

    (vi)   Step 6: Run end-of-day process

    (vii)   etc.

(e) Test threads should contain a sufficient number of test cases to adequately test that business process through the system.

(f) Note that there should be two test threads per business process – one that contains legitimate data to test all legitimate paths through the system and one that deliberately tries to find flaws in the system's implementation of the business process.

(g) Lengthy test threads should be avoided. Some test threads may therefore need to be split into more manageable chunks. For example, testing all on-line queries in a single test thread should be avoided, try to clump the queries into logical groupings so that the results of one query can be tested against the output of another.

(h) Note that Computer Aided System Test (CAST) tools can be used to capture the script once and replay it many times. This is especially useful for systems with long lifespans.

(i) Also as new errors are found, new steps in the test thread should be added to test for those errors. In this way, the test thread can evolve into a comprehensive test document.

3   Tick lists (optional):

(a) For simple one-function testing (e.g. unit testing), a tick list may be preferable to a test thread.

(b) Tick lists are lists of simple checks to perform whereby the tester gives a tick or cross for each check as he/she performs the test.

(c) An example of a tick list for a single screen is as follows:

- [ ] performs as per design specification
- [ ] performs as per user guide or help screen
- [ ] does not allow invalid data
- [ ] does not allow invalid keys
- [ ] screen and report header is per standard
- [ ] screen and report layout is per standard
- [ ] screen and column labels correct and per standard
- [ ] screen and column labels match field and column content
- [ ] save works
- [ ] cancel works
- [ ] response times acceptable

4   Test thread coverage (optional):

(a) For particularly complex modules, it may be relevant to get a printout of the sourcecode. This could then be sidelined to indicate sections of code that are to be tested. Thread and step references could be added for traceability.

(b) This method can assist in the production of test threads by making the tester step through the code to identify all the sequences, loops and conditional logic.

(c) If this approach is adopted, it is important to decide whether this is a 'throw-away' document done once or whether the module merits this approach to be sustained. If it is to be sustained then it is important to refresh the source-code listing and sidelines every time it comes into the test environment.

5   Test thread dependency:

(a) In complex systems, the output of one test thread may form the input of one of more other test threads. For example, orders set up in the 'Order Entry' test thread could be used in the 'Invoicing' test thread and the 'New Orders Query' test thread. There is a need to produce a document/diagram which shows which test threads feed into which other test threads.

(b) Dependencies should be identified as 'hard' or 'soft'. 'Hard' dependencies mean that the previous thread must succeed before this thread can take place. 'Soft' dependencies mean that the results of the previous thread could be used but are not essential. In our example above, the 'Invoicing' thread has a hard dependency on the 'Order Entry' thread. The 'New Orders Query' thread could still be run (even if nothing appears in the query) and hence its dependency is 'soft'.

(c) There should be as few 'hard' dependencies as possible since it is desirable to test as much of the system as possible in one test run. By definition, 'hard' dependencies mean that the failure of one thread prevents the testing of its dependent threads. This has the effect of holding up testing. In short, it is better to test as comprehensively as possible so that errors can be found early. Testing dependencies may mean that faults are found much later than desirable.

(d) The dependency document/diagram can be used to produce a test plan (see Test schedule section below).

6   Test schedule (also known as a test plan):

(a) This is a composite document outlining how a test run is to be performed.

(b) It takes the form of a matrix chart (see example).

(c) It should show on a day-by-day basis:
   (i)   which test threads are being performed in the whole test-run
   (ii) which test thread steps are being performed on each day
   (iii) who is performing which step on each thread each day.

Test day	1	2	3	4	5	6
Actual (target) date	20/3	21/3	24/3	25/3	26/3	27/3
Threads						
Order entry	1–2 (Paul)	3–6 (Paul)		7–9 (Paul)		
Invoicing			1–6 (Kate)	7–10 (Kate)	11 (Kate)	12 (Kate)
End of day	1 (Ops)	1 (Ops)	1 (Ops)	1 (Ops)	1 (Ops)	

(d) Once a test schedule has been produced it can be reused by revising the actual dates entered.

(e) A significant advantage of this approach is that it shows how long it takes to complete a set of tests. This can be used in the overall planning process. It can also be used to show the impact a failed thread will have on the test-run timescales.

7 Test run summary report:

    (a) Each time a test run is completed (whether failed or successful) a report should be produced to show:

        (i) which threads were run (from the test schedule)

        (ii) whether the thread passed or failed (and by whom on what date)

        (iii) a list of incidents raised with appropriate error-weighting (see Incident sheet section below).

8 Incident sheet:

    (a) For each error detected, an incident sheet should be produced containing:

        (i) unique incident number for tracking purposes

        (ii) date tested and test thread and step reference

        (iii) description of error

        (iv) error severity level (see checklist 7.10 'How to prioritize errors and grade the acceptance of functions').

    (b) This sheet should travel with the system function(s) that are to be amended.

    (c) When the function is released back into testing, the following details should be completed:

        (i) name of fixer and date fixed

        (ii) effort spent in fixing

        (iii) description of fix

        (iv) comment as to how error occurred and, if applicable, why not trapped earlier.

    (d) Naturally the fix may not work hence the above information should be captured each time the incident passes into testing, i.e. a new incident should not be raised, or if it is, this information should be transcribed onto the new incident.

9 Test run statistics:

    (a) For a series of test runs, some statistics should be produced to show the overall impact of the testing and fixing effort.

    (b) A number of different measures can be used:

        (i) test graph – number of errors found on y-axis, time (in days or weeks) on x-axis; shows whether things are getting bad or worse

        (ii) weighted Test Graph – as above but the errors are weighted according to severity to show really how good or bad things are getting

        (iii) test effectiveness measure = (errors found in review)/(errors found in review + errors found in testing + errors found in operation) – the closer to 1 the cheaper the system

        (iv) system quality measure = minor errors/major errors – a good quality system will make this a small number.

Definitions/techniques

None.

Next steps

After each testing run, it is important to review the testing records and statistics with the testing team:

- What went well?
- What went badly?
- How could the testing effort be improved?
- Outside of testing, what else should be put in place to improve the quality of future systems?
- Are there any additional tests that should be added to the test schedule for the next test run?

For more information on generating test threads see checklist 7.7 'Where to get test data from for application testing'.

7.7 Where to get test data from for application testing

Type: Analysis

Checklist description

Generating test data is at the heart of the testing process, but it is also sometimes the most difficult activity to get to grips with. Comprehensive test data leads to comprehensive testing but where does that data come from? This checklist suggests some of the sources for test data.

Checklist

Business Process Documentation
- Look in business documentation for:
  - key acceptance criteria – this will establish key items to test
  - key business transactions – this will establish what the test threads should be
  - types of events or triggers of a business process – this can establish initiating data that should be used (e.g. a 'Purchase Order received' trigger identifies a source of initiating data: purchase orders)
  - process diagrams produce thread scripts. This can also be used to give a thread an overall structure including handovers from one test thread to another.

System Documentation
- Look in system documentation for:
  - entities and entity subtypes – can show fundamental types of transaction not just Create Customer, Create order but also create Customer who is a private individual and Create customer who is a company etc.
  - key processes – can be used to identify individual test threads. Also if input/output data items are identified these can be used to build complex cases based on the different values the data can take
  - key paths – can be used to build the steps in a test thread
  - system interfaces – can be used to identify handover data for testing
  - menu structures and short-cut keys – can be used to identify individual transaction threads and separate areas to test
  - key areas of company exposure – these should be tested more thoroughly.
- Consider non functional requirements   build up tests that cover.
  - performance – number of users, volumes
  - controls – can month-end be run twice? Can a customer or order be input twice?
  - restart/recovery procedure – can it be followed? Does it work? Does it cater for all kinds of crash?

Develop 'outliers'
- So far the above sources of test data have identified what is expected by the developers, i.e. testing for success. However, testing should also include tests for the unexpected and tests for failure.
- Use a brainstorming technique to develop 'what ifs' – for example:
  - what if the form or delivery is incomplete?
  - what if delivery quantity is greater than order quantity?

- – what if it's a delivery without an order?
- – what if batch totals don't match?
- – what if mandatory data is missing?
- – what do you do with stuff written in the margins?
- Quite a lot of this type of data is 'real world' – what could happen in the real world? Essentially the tester needs to test how the system will be used not how the developer thinks it may be used.

Live data

- Live data can be taken from the existing live system and loaded into the test systems database (or converted into it). Also real order forms, request forms etc. can be photocopied and made available to the test team.
- However, there is a lot of debate over whether live data should be used to test a system. It needs careful weighing. Here are some points for and against.
- Advantages:
  - – readily available
  - – high number of cases (volume)
  - – breadth of cases (case-types)
  - – may contain more variants than can be generated manually
  - – often the effect of time and multiple updates is lacking in artificial test data.
- Disadvantages:
  - – too much volume may obscure where problems are
  - – possibility of mix-up with 'live system' increases dramatically and may not be worth the risk
  - – Data Protection Act issues
  - – may not test all the paths of a new system – so false sense of security
  - – necessitates 'test system' (CPU, disk space etc.) of similar size to 'live system' to run tests
  - – may require a large test team to input 'live' transactions

Definitions/techniques

For a more information on brainstorming, see checklist 2.6 'Different ways of generating solutions for a problem'.

Next steps

See also checklist 7.8 'General tests to apply to a screen'.

7.8   General tests to apply to a screen

Type: QA

Checklist description

This checklist is a comprehensive 'tick list' for checking the quality of a screen. It can be used to ensure nothing has been missed in the building of a screen component.

Checklist

Screen header

☐ standard layout with correct and relevant information

☐ module and version number displayed for support-call use

☐ help screen available

☐ correct spelling, spacing.

Cursor movement

☐ correct and appropriate starting position on screen (may be dependent on previous screen(s))

☐ correct and appropriate 'next field' sequence (may be dependent on previous field input).

Function keys, icons, menus and buttons

☐ have the desired effect

☐ have acceptable performance and response time

☐ have acceptable 'sensitivity' (e.g. down-arrow button scrolls right amount of text)

☐ consistent with other screens

☐ consistent with industry standards.

Field input (see field input checklist)

☐ mandatory/optional data enforced and is reasonable (and user is shown when mandatory data is required)

☐ valid data accepted (including valid combinations of data)

☐ invalid data rejected (including invalid combinations of data)

☐ error messages rude or helpful

☐ scrolling left/right, up/down is appropriate to size and position of field

☐ correct spelling, spacing and alignment of field label

☐ field label suitably identifies field type or field input mask (e.g. date as dd/mm/yyyy?)

☐ correct alignment of field input mask

☐ correct display and use of default if nothing entered.

'Save' function

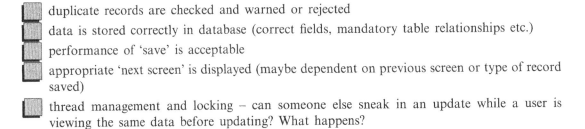

☐ duplicate records are checked and warned or rejected

☐ data is stored correctly in database (correct fields, mandatory table relationships etc.)

☐ performance of 'save' is acceptable

☐ appropriate 'next screen' is displayed (maybe dependent on previous screen or type of record saved)

☐ thread management and locking – can someone else sneak in an update while a user is viewing the same data before updating? What happens?

Definitions/techniques

None.

Next steps

Valid/invalid data checking mentioned in the tick list is a detailed area of testing in itself – see checklist 7.9 'How to generate test data for screen fields (domains)'.

7.9 How to generate test data for screen fields (domains)

Type: To do

Checklist description

When presented with a screen to test, it can be difficult to know where to start. This checklist gives some ideas as to how to analyse screen fields for generating test data.

Checklist

1   For all character fields, try:

- A–Z, 0–9
- mix of upper/lower case – how entered, how stored, how searched, how displayed
- special characters – spaces, commas, brackets, tabs, question marks, asterisks – others?
- people's names with special characters, e.g. O'Brian, Piggott-Smith, Charles the Second, Acme Ltd (London branch).

2   For all date fields, try:

- two- or four-digit years and date-window boundaries
- lower/upper limit (how far in the past or future?)
- format dd/mm/yy or mm/dd/yy etc. (international defaults?)
- date component separators, e.g. dd/mm/yy or dd-mm-yy or ddmmyy etc. What if a duplicate separator is entered 2//2/2000?
- allow time entry, e.g. (1/1/2000:23:14)
- special dates checked for – bank holidays, year-end, tax-year, Feb. 29th.

3   For all numeric fields, try:

- integer-only values, floating-point values, fixed-decimal-point values
- more than one decimal point
- use of commas in the correct place (e.g. 1,000) and in the incorrect place (e.g. 1,00)
- upper/lower limits
- negative signs – before/after the input number
- currency format – use of commas, use of fixed decimal point and how to handle if no decimal point entered, are large denomination currencies expected?
- use of decimal places in calculations – rounding errors – what is acceptable?
- special characters – spaces, commas, brackets, tabs, question marks, asterisks, currency symbols – others?
- A–Z, a–z.

4   Identify mandatory/optional fields:

- try storing nothing using:
  - spaces
  - tab and back-tab
  - Enter/Return
  - ESC
  - up/down/left/right arrow.
  - click or double-click on another field.

5   Identify dependent fields:
- check all the valid combinations
- generate invalid pairings
- what happens if the fields are populated in reverse order?
- what happens if fields are populated in correct order and then an earlier field is corrected or blanked?

6   Attempt some brainstorming for values:
- what happens if this field has an error in it?
- what could I enter in this field that would give the system serious problems?
- what could I enter in this field that would give interface systems serious problems?

Definitions/techniques

Date-window boundaries – some systems allow two-digit year entries which convert the date into a four-digit year based on a date boundary. For example, if date boundary is 1/1/1970, all two-digit years less than 70 are deemed to be twenty-first century, e.g. 1/1/01 is 1/1/2001 but 1/1/99 is 1/1/1999.

Field dependency – if the values of one field determine what can be entered in another field.

Next steps

Produce a list of valid and non-valid values to test against each domain. This can be reused across many screens. Also see checklist 7.8 'General tests to apply to a screen'.

7.10 How to prioritize errors and grade the acceptance of functions

Type: Analysis

Checklist description

When testing, it quickly becomes apparent that all errors should not be treated equally. Whilst there may be some minor annoyances, there are also 'show stoppers'. Even within serious errors, there may be a 'pecking order' of fixes. Hence as part of testing it is important to priortize errors.

Below are two ways of categorizing errors. The first list is for individual errors, i.e. assign a number category to a discovered defect. The second list can be used to grade individual functions within the system.

Checklist

Grading of errors

1　No impact – bad spelling, incorrect alignment.

2　Minor impact – misleading information, superfluous information, truncation of field information.

3　Medium impact – legal actions disallowed, illegal actions allowed, sometimes works and sometimes doesn't.

4　Serious impact – loss or corruption of data.

5　Very serious impact – misposts one or two transactions.

6　Extreme impact – misposts almost all transactions.

7　Unrecoverable error – system introduces errors which cannot be undone.

8　Viral error – system introduces errors into other systems which cannot be undone.

9　Catastrophic failure – system shuts down or prevents access or use.

10　Extreme catastrophic failure – system shuts other systems down.

Grading of functions

1　Never fails to work.

2　Works well.

3　Barely works.

4　Does not work.

Definitions/techniques

None.

Next steps

The first list can be used to prioritize remedial work whilst the second list can be used to determine which functions require potential upgrading or remedial work. This second list could be used to assess overall acceptability and what is required to make the system acceptable.

7.11   Power testing 1 – checking the underlying database

Type: Analysis

Checklist description

Sometimes testing can focus only on the visible – what's on a screen or report. Under the covers of many applications is a database. The 'garbage in, garbage out' rule would dictate that if something is not right with the database, it will show up somewhere. But sometimes it can take a long time for a corruption in the database to show up.

Since one of the objectives of testing is to detect errors as soon as possible (and before a live implementation), a 'power' tester should employ the range of tests and techniques covered in this checklist to discover errors by turning attention to the underlying database.

Checklist

SQL technique	Used for
Bulk copy out	Use to confirm correct data updates, i.e. capture the pre- and post-conditions by copying the data to an ASCII file and doing a file compare once the test has been completed.
SUM/COUNT	Use to ensure: • full range of test cases is present in the DB • imported data has properly converted • derived data is correct (especially partial updates) • as a pre-/post-condition for data recovery, e.g. take total, crash db, recover db, take total, ensure totals match • can show missing or duplicated data. Counts could be: • sums of all financial fields • counts of rows • sums of integer key values • sum of first character position of 'e', say in text fields
MAX	Use to ensure that last updated date on columns for all critical tables is not after the last recovered position (i.e. a recovery test).
NULL/NOT NULL function	Ensure that mandatory data is present.
Left/Right join	Ensure that mandatory entities are present – can show partial-update problem.
Count/Group by/Having	Ensure that duplicates have been disallowed where applicable.
Len function	Check for field truncation.
Query path	Can ensure complex SQL has no many-to-many joins (Cartesian product).

Definitions/techniques

Cartesian product – a mathematical term referring to multiplying two matrices together. Since relational database theory is based on matrix theory, this term is sometimes used for many-to-many table joins. Specifically, for each row in one table, all the rows in another table are added to the output. Hence if there is a bad join between Table A with N rows and Table B with M rows, the resulting output will be M × N rows.

Next steps

See also the next two 'power testing' checklists.

7.12   Power testing 2 – thrashing and crashing the system

Type: To do

Checklist description

One approach in testing is to test it to destruction. Only then can the real flaws of the system be found. The fact is that unless the tester finds them, the end-user eventually will with all the business risk that that entails.

This checklist is intended to inspire the 'power tester' to find the flaws in the system by providing a sample 'hit list'.

Checklist

Session thrashing
- Check login speed with multiple login (i.e. to simulate Monday morning at 9am).
- Check logoff speed with multiple logoff (i.e. to simulate Friday night at 5pm).
- Keep logging on users until login process slows down – i.e. what is the session-handling limit for this application architecture?

Volume thrashing
- Get as many sessions as possible (see above) to run the most resource-hungry function or transaction.
- Get as many sessions as possible to run the most common-usage function.
- For each of these tests, monitor for the following:
  - At what volume can the system cope without any degradation of performance?
  - At what volume does system performance start to degrade?
  - At what volume does the system break?
- Compare the answers to these against expected peaks and troughs per day, week, year and special circumstance (e.g. market boom) and the expected mix of transactions.
- Can the system cope with zero volume?
- Try defining the database with a small or non-existent fill factor.
  - What happens when the database or data tables go over its fill factor?
  - What is the expected fill factor and expected growth of the database, i.e. when will the fill factor be reached?
  - Is there some automatic or manual process that detects running out of fill factor early enough to be corrected? Run a test to ensure this works.

Recovery thrashing
- What happens if you recover it twice – double updates or transactions?
- What happens if you roll through transactions – any missing updates or transactions?
- Check whether recovery has removed any indexes or pointers.
- After recovery, check whether table relationships are out of step (i.e. one table updated the other not).
- Does recovery successfully restore status of temporary files and tables? What about system/registry settings?
- Does recovery successfully restore status of import and extract files?
- What is the status of interface systems after recovery – do they need recovering too?

- Check all the file last changed date/time stamps to ensure they are consistent with the recovered position.
- Check the row last changed date/time stamp. Are they consistent with the recovered position? Does the change in system date matter?

Hardware

- If one component fails, does the system become unusable?
- What is the resilience and robustness of the system?
    - Is there a suitable level of redundancy to take up the slack?
    - Is hardware failure invisible to the users?

Definitions/techniques

None.

Next steps

See previous and next 'power testing' checklists.

7.13   Power testing 3 – checking the business controls

Type: To do

Checklist description

One of the problems with testing environments is that the tests are constructed and conducted in a non-live environment. This can lead to a concentration on whether the functionality of the system is correct and ignores whether the system will correctly fit the business process.

This checklist provides guidance for the 'power tester' on how to look beyond the system at the surrounding business process controls.

Checklist

Function/Data access controls checks
- Draw up a matrix of user types, functions and data segments.
- Check for each user type that:
  - they can access the functions permitted
  - they cannot access the functions disallowed
  - they can only see the data for which they are responsible
  - they cannot request a report or query which will contain data for which they are not responsible.
- Test the report and function which records:
  - illegal login attempts
  - illegal function attempts.

Business process sequence checks
- If there is an implied sequence of actions or a branched-sequence of actions then test:
  - actions are only allowed when they should be allowed
  - actions aren't disallowed when they should be allowed
  - actions are allowed when they should be disallowed
  - specifically on Internet/intranet applications test for the use of forward/backward browser buttons taking the user to allowed/disallowed pages
  - specifically on internet/intranet application test whether pages can be requested and accessed by guesswork.

Auditing and activity logging control checks
- Check that all actions required to be logged are being logged.
- Check whether the audit report captures enough significant activity – test for:
  - report on changes
  - report on effects of changes
  - report on unusual values or volumes
  - report on attempts to gain access which were rejected
  - report on how the batch run was completed (including errors and resubmissions).

General checks
- Authority checks

     – Does the system support the business process need for separation of duties (i.e. a doer and an authorizer)?

     – Does the system seek confirmation before certain actions are carried out?

- Completeness
  - Are all actions recorded?
  - Are there any actions that are invisible (e.g. DBA update of a table)?
- Accuracy
  - Are all critical calculations correct?
- Integrity
  - Are all the transactions and postings consistently accurate?
  - Are there any partial updates which require manual intervention?

Definitions/techniques

None.

Next steps

See previous two 'power testing' checklists.

8
System implementation checklists

8.1 Change-auditing and change-capacity assessment – how to see the big picture

Type: Analysis

Checklist description

Whenever a new computer system is implemented in an organization, it is really the business processes which are changing. It's almost impossible to keep everything else the same and just bring in a new computer. Otherwise what's the point of making the change in the first place? However, implementing changes in the business are often far more complex than the installation of a new computer system.

This checklist is intended to help generate an overview of what is changing in the business, how to quantify the level of change and whether the change can be 'absorbed' by the business.

Checklist

Change audit

Change can affect some fundamental structures of the business. It is important to 'audit' each fundamental structure for change in order to produce a change plan.

(a) Create a table as shown below. (Note that for big changes this audit may need to be done on, say, a business-process by business-process basis.)

(b) Show how the proposed business change will affect each of the items below.

- Power and organization structure.
    - Roles and responsibilities.
        - Who will it affect?
        - What will they do that they didn't do before?
        - What won't they do that they did before?
    - Management processes and accountability (including number of management levels).
        - Who will be the controller of that activity and how will they monitor and control it?
    - Operational processes and procedures (and standards).
        - Who else needs to know of the change?
        - How do we communicate that to them?
    - Jobs and skills
        - Are any jobs or skills no longer required?
        - Are there new jobs or skills that need to be acquired?
- Reward structure.
    - Measurement, metrics and benefits.
        - How will we know if the change was successful?
        - What new measuring devices do we need?
        - What is a bad, good, average metric?
- Recognition, incentives, rewards.
    - What 'carrots' can be put in place to make it successful?
    - What 'carrots' can be put in place to keep it successful?
    - Are any punishments required?

- Information technology.
  - Data and systems.
    - What new technology is being introduced?
    - How much more data is to be captured to run the new system?
- Company culture.
  - Shared values.
    - How will the change affect our shared values (e.g. moving from a 'family' atmosphere to a 'corporate' one)
    - Will it be perceived as hypocritical? Are we being consistent?
  - Attitude towards quality and adding value.
    - How does the change affect our view of ourselves, our customers, our suppliers?
    - How will it enable people to serve our customers better?
- Company direction.
  - Policies.
    - Does the change fit current policy? Are the two at odds? What should be done?

(c) Add a sequence and priority to the actions.

An Example:

Structure + Element	Current	New and who is affected	What needs to happen to whom by whom to move from current to new	Sequence	Priority
Role change	Stores and Purchasing are separate depts	Purchasing responsibility (currently Dave in Accounts) will move to Stores (Mgr Bill)	– Bill will be offered Stores and Purchasing Mgr (Exec)	2	High
			– Additional admin support for Bill required (HR)	10	Medium
			– Dave released from Purchasing, will continue as Accounts Clerk (ACs)	10	Low
Management procedures	As above	As above	– Bill will be required to produce monthly purchasing reports and budgets to Accounts (ACs)	8	Medium
Operational procedures	As above	As above	– All Purchase orders will go to Stores so new procedure to be developed and launched to all with purchasing authority (Training)	4	High
Jobs and skills	As above	As above	– Bill trained in new system (Training)	3	High
			– Bill trained in Purchasing practices (ACs)	4	High

Reward structure	As above	As above	– 6 month pay review with Bill being offered Management grade 2 (Exec/HR)	1	Medium
			– bonus if Bill reduces purchasing turnaround from 4 to 2 weeks (Exec/HR)	2	Medium
Information technology	As above	As above	– Inventory system will have a purchasing and goods receipt module added (IT)	1	High
etc.					

Assessing capacity for change

If the level of change overwhelms an organization then there is serious risk to the organization of people becoming disaffected. It is vital to assess an organization's capacity for change:

(a) Taking the action column of the previous table and list all the individuals and departments (whether they are the initiator or receiver of the action), the action, the sequence and the priority.

(b) Order this column by name (and by sequence or priority within name) so all the actions to/from an individual or department are listed together.

(c) Looking at the actions against each name (their sequence and priority), note the following:

- Level of disruption to that individual, department or team – high, medium, low
- Value or significance of the activity to the change goal – high, medium, low
- Likely attitude of individual or team towards the activity – reluctant, ambivalent, embracing.

(d) Determine the capacity for change:

- Is there enough time allowed for this activity?
- Are there enough staff for this activity?
- Do the staff possess the correct skills for this activity?
- Are there any external factors that have to be addressed before the change can take place (e.g. consultation with unions, signing of contracts etc.)?
- Does the activity fit with the current culture? Is there enough motivation for this activity? Is the management style suitable to managing this type of activity?

(e) Determine the capacity for change over the change timescale:

- What is the implication if the change occurs during:
  - financial year-end or accounts audit?
  - tax year-end, VAT reporting quarter?
  - peak customer demand period (e.g. ice-cream sales in the summer)?
  - stock-taking period?
  - holiday periods (Christmas, New Year, school holidays etc.)?
  - external events (political election, Budget etc.)?

Managing the change capacity

From the above, if there are doubts over whether capacity is sufficient for an individual, department or team to absorb the change, a number of strategies can be adopted:

- Increase the number of staff (with the use of temporary or contracted labour) – note that this is not an overnight process!
- Revise the change-implementation timescales (but check that you have not extended the change into a 'busy period').
- Conduct more pre-change consultation and communication exercises.
- Remove some non-critical activities.
- Scale back the level of change.

Definitions/techniques

None.

Next steps

Once the change-audit and capacity assessment have been made, it is possible to draw up a change-plan. This should indicate what is to be done to whom by whom for when. It is also possible to show the resources and dependencies of all the activities.

Note, however, that this is only the first-cut plan. It needs to be communicated, at which point other factors may be brought to light.

The two real keys of effective change are communication and involvement. As a rule people don't like change and people like change forced upon them even less. One method of moving people from A to B is:

- show them A
- tell them why they can't stay at A (i.e. what is the catalyst for change?)
- show them B (or involve them in picking B)
- tell them why the organization needs to get to B (i.e. what does it lead to?)
- tell them what were the alternatives to B and why they were rejected
- ask them how to get from A to B
- if there are many alternatives to get from A to B, help them to sort the alternatives into a preferred method
- do the change audit and capacity management on the final outcome of previous step
- show them the results and get them to refine them as necessary
- keep looping with the previous two steps until agreement is reached and change is achievable.

If shown A and B and shown 'why', most people will be happy to help with the 'how'.

8.2   Things to plan for in an implementation

Type: Analysis

Checklist description

You can build the most wonderful system in the world, but it won't do the business any good if it's badly implemented. Good implementation requires careful planning. It is the point where the business is most exposed to risk so it is effectively both an exercise in logistics and risk management.

This checklist can help to identify areas that require logistics. However, on top of this checklist, you should ask yourself, 'What else can go wrong? What are my other risks?'

Checklist

Installation

1   Roll-out plan:
- Big-bang vs phased.
  - How easy is it to support old and new systems together?
  - What is least risk to the business?
  - What is the business expecting?
- Delivery.
  - Will the technical architecture be in place in time?
  - Will software and hardware be installed simultaneously?
- Conversion.
  - Is there a clear success criteria and a fallback position if the initial attempt fails?
  - Have the conversion programs been written?
  - Has the conversion been adequately tested?
  - Has all the data been identified for conversion?
  - Is all the data to be converted or is it a gradual take-on? (See also checklist 8.7 'How to do a data conversion'.)
  - Is data cleansing required? Will this be automated or manual?
  - Is it clear how data will be copied from one system to the other (e.g. transport media, transport devices, e.g. tape drives etc.)?
  - Are additional staff required – e.g. rekeying of data, correcting of data, completion of data for new system?
  - Is there a clear success criteria and a fallback position if the initial attempt fails?

2   Integration testing (see also: Section 7, QA and testing checklists)
- Test harness
  - Set up:
    - Is a separate testing environment required (i.e. additional machines, disks, PCs, cabling etc.)?
    - Are there additional test personnel required?
    - Who should conduct the testing?
  - Coverage:
    - Can the whole core infrastructure be tested?

- • Can all systems communicate using the networks?
- • Can the systems work together effectively?
- • Is all critical functionality in the first release?
- • Are all critical functions adequately tested?
- • Does the testing include performance tests?
- • Is the performance suitable and sustainable?
  - – Maintenance:
    - • Can new or changed requirements be added to a test plan?
    - • Are tests repeatable?

3 Business preparation:
- • Education
  - – Has sufficient training been provided? (See checklist 8.4 'How to build a training course'.)
  - – What documentation do you need to run this system?
    - • Suitable reference guides.
    - • Suitable user and reference guides as well as help screens.
    - • Operational schedules, sequences and procedures (regular, irregular, backup).
    - • Disaster recovery procedures.
    - • Incident and change-control procedures.
  - – Are there trained support staff on hand to help?
  - – Are there computer operations tasks to be performed?
  - – Have computer operations been trained?
  - – Is there an operator manual? And a quick-reference guide?
- • Work methods
  - – What documentation do you need to run the new or revised business process?
    - • Are new forms or stationery required?
    - • Are there sufficient printers for the adequate throughput?
    - • Is there sufficient filing space?
    - • Is the filing space accessible?
  - – Have the changes to work methods been made clear?
  - – Are additional staff required to implement the revised business process? When are they available?
  - – Are additional staff required to run the system?
  - – Is it clear what improvements are expected?
  - – If problems arise, have workarounds been devised?

4 Environment:
- • Machine
  - – Is the machine location and cooling system suitable? Do they present any health and safety risks?
  - – Does the machine need to be in a physically secure area?
  - – Is an uninterruptible power supply installed, tested and working?
  - – Has cabling been completed and connected to appropriate office computers?
- • Key software (operating system, DBMS, other)
  - – Ensure that all versions are known.
  - – Check that licences have been obtained and that licence strings (if required) are

available. Do the licences permit the expected number of users to access the system?
- Check that the software has been installed correctly in the correct directory structure
- Check that DB build scripts have been included and loading of lookups and/or predefined values (e.g. default first user name, corporate defaults) has been done.

● Other
- Fire-detection and fire-fighting equipment has been installed and relevant parties trained?
- Office space reorganization is complete?
- Other health and safety requirements have been checked?

Security

1 Access:

● Application
- Are all legal users registered?
- Are there specific levels of access, e.g. read-only vs update?
- Are there procedures in place for adding and removing users?
- Who is responsible for maintaining the register?
- Is all access under password control?
- How often must passwords be changed?
- What happens if users forget their passwords?
- Do all logon screens state that unauthorized access is illegal?
- Who controls special stationery (e.g. cheques, purchase orders etc.)? Does the system provide for the alignment of special stationery before printing?

● Network
- How easy is it to hack into the system?
- Are there sufficient safeguards to prevent illegal access (e.g. firewalls)?

● Operating environment
- Are users protected from accessing the operating system?
- If a software error occurs, which area is the user left in?
- Do all users have access to DBMS, files, directories, programs that they need? Have they got the correct read, write, delete, execute permissions?
- How is the granting or revoking access at this level to be controlled?

2 Environment:

● Theft
- Can the software be pirated?
- Can the data be pirated? Should data be encrypted?
- How secure are downloads, backups etc.?
- What precautions have been taken to protect the hardware?

● Work area
- Are there any dangerous cables trailing in the floor?
- Is the equipment near potentially harmful water, heating etc.?

● Operating system
- Can illegal software be loaded?
- Can non-standard software be loaded?

- Is there sufficient virus protection?
- Availability of a console log to track what has been done, by when, by whom?

3 Information:
- Confidential waste
  - Are staff aware of their responsibility regarding reports etc.?
  - Has a method of disposing of reports been implemented?
- Data Protection Act
  - Do we comply with the Act regarding data capture and usage?
  - Are we appropriately registered for data usage?

Support

1 Application:
- Help desk
  - Do users know who to call in case of problems? Is the help-desk procedure known to all? How will you prevent 'back-door' access to experts which could undermine the help desk?
  - What is the service level for urgent/non-urgent calls? Can the help desk handle expected volumes?
  - What level of support is provided? Are there procedures in place to deal with prioritization and categorization of calls? Are the help-desk operatives suitably trained to be a front-line support that end-users can be confident with?
  - Is there a clear escalation path from front line to system expert?
  - What happens for user access both application and OpSys, DB, network level? Who can ask for user access changes? How is it done? Who checks it? Who authorizes it?
    - Addition of new users.
    - Deletion of ex-users.
    - Reinstating forgotten passwords.
    - Changing users access profile.
- If external suppliers are involved, who is the contact point? Do you have appropriate service-level agreements with them (see SLA section) which includes an escalation path with them?
- Software
  - How are software errors to be resolved? When errors occur, what is the method of identifying them? How are they recorded? Who records them? What happens next? Is there any distinction between the level of error as to what happens next?
  - Are the change and fix procedures understood by all parties? Is there a clear software change and release procedure?
  - Does the software release system cater for emergencies and can it filter out the annoying but insignificant changes? Who decides what are urgent/non-urgent bug fixes?
  - What if there are new/changed requirements?
  - How are releases to be tested?
  - Who is responsible for changing, testing and releasing?
  - Can software be released to all sites simultaneously?
  - Can multiple versions of an application co-exist?

- Operations
  - How are overnight jobs kicked off?
  - Who carries out backups and when? Who controls the backup media? What is the cycle of backup media reuse?
  - Who is responsible for disk management?
  - How is disk management and performance tuning done?
  - How are these functions done on a remote system?
  - Where are backups stored?

2 Environment:

- Hardware, OpSys and DB
  - When maintenance needs to occur, who will identify it? Who does it? Who checks it? When can it be done?
  - When will upgrades be performed?
  - How will upgrades be tested?
  - When is the best time for the service to be unavailable?
  - How will off-site servicing be performed?

Configuration

1 Change control:

- Risk
  - Can proposed changes be analysed for their impact?
  - Who is responsible for sign-off of a major change?
  - How flexible is the configuration to major changes?
  - How will new developments be introduced?
- Interfaces
  - How is access to databases to be monitored?
  - What is the procedure for requesting access?
  - How will changes between two systems be co-ordinated?
  - Who decides mandatory changes between two systems?
  - How are changes to data definitions communicated to all?
- Version control
  - How will versions be controlled in multiple-live versions?
  - How will many versions to be brought into line?

2 Environment:

- Hardware, OpSys and DB
  - Who is responsible for each element?
  - How are they to be co-ordinated?
  - How are configuration changes authorized?
  - What stops elements being changed without authorization?
- Languages and compilers
  - How are these to be upgraded?
  - Who owns these elements?
  - Are they upward compatible?
  - Can multiple versions run in the same environment?

Contingency

1   Application:
- Data
    - How will remote backups be taken and stored?
    - Will the systems allow the restoring of an old backup?
    - If data corruption occurs, how will this be fixed remotely? If data needs to be changed outside of using the application, who does it? Who checks it? Who can ask for it to be done? When can it be done?
    - What if data is lost, what reports exist to help rekey data?
- Software
    - What procedures exist for fast uptime in case of emergency?
    - How will all branches be notified of an error at head office?
    - What happens when batch-run fails, who gets called out? Who fixes it? Who checks the fixes? Who authorizes it? What happens next day?

2   Environment:
- Hardware, OpSys, DB
    - What recovery routines are in place for each element?
    - What is the recovery routine for each core system?
    - How reliant is the business on each core system?
    - Can a core system be down with little critical impact?
    - What response times have we negotiated with suppliers?
- Network and ODBC
    - What if all/part of the network is unavailable?
    - What response times have we negotiated with suppliers?
- Disaster recovery
    - Which elements must be recovered?
    - What is the required timescale for critical elements?
    - How much of the network must be present?
    - What items must be present in a standby site?
    - How many individuals must be relocated as a necessity?
    - Can certain functions be made available from homes?

Definitions/techniques

None.

Next steps

Incidentally, one risk that may need to be assessed and managed carefully is where there is a high project dependence on certain individuals. Someone walking out at the wrong moment in an implementation can seriously jeopardize the project's success. Some of the strategies to retain key staff are:

- change their contract to a 3-month notice period
- pay an incentive to stay or agree a large end-of-project bonus
- stay aware of the individual's personal goals, ambitions and objectives, and be prepared to be flexible (e.g. flexible working arrangements, additional training, 'perks', job status etc.)

- ultimately, you have to out-think your opponent's incentive scheme. Your opponent is the employer who wants to lure your key person away from you.

This checklist can be used to drive activities towards an eventual launch date. However, as that date arrives a smaller checklist may be required – see checklist 8.3 'Adopting the NASA go/no-go list'.

8.3 Adopting the NASA go/no-go list

Type: QA

Checklist description

As the day of system launch approaches, it is worthwhile adopting the NASA go/no-go approach with key people owning each part of the go/no-go list. At each implementation meeting, these key questions are asked. It is only if all the items are 'go' should the system be launched.

Note that it is best not to increase this list by too much – it is meant to be a summary and not too detailed. If detailed lists are required, they should be implemented as sub-lists by each key individual for their own use in answering these questions.

Checklist

System acceptance go/no-go

- [ ] Have all the acceptance criteria been agreed?
- [ ] Has the system met the criteria (through testing)?
- [ ] Has the system been accepted?
- [ ] Is the data conversion complete?
- [ ] Is the data conversion satisfactory?

System installation go/no-go

- [ ] Is the system (hardware, network, devices, OpSys, DBMS, application software) complete?
- [ ] Has it been correctly and completely installed?
- [ ] Are all user profiles installed with correct permissions?

Business environment go/no-go

- [ ] Are the users ready?
- [ ] Is the training of users complete?
- [ ] Have any new legislation or practices come into effect that affect the system which has not already been trapped?
- [ ] Is now the right time for launch? Are we still in a launch window?

External factors go/no-go

- [ ] Do the 'suppliers' (including interface systems) know what they have agreed to supply?
- [ ] Are they ready to supply them?

Contingency plan go/no-go

- [ ] If an abort is sounded, can the contingency plan come into immediate effect?
- [ ] Are there any dependencies on the contingency plan that are not in place?

Definitions/techniques

None.

Next steps

If any of the answers above are 'No' then obviously there is a risk to the business if the system is launched. For safety sake, it would be better not to launch if there is any doubt on the above issues.

However, a launch can sometimes be contemplated provided there is adequate management of the risk, e.g. year-end reporting can be agreed to be delivered at a later date if the year-end is 10 months away.

8.4 How to build a training course

Type: To do

Checklist description

Like all the activities of software development and deployment, to be successful, training requires careful planning. In fact, the training programme for a new system needs to be handled as if it were its own development. As such it needs to pass through various development stages:

- user requirements analysis
- course structure and design
- course build
- training roll-out plan
- course maintenance.

This checklist offers some of the steps to create effective training. Note, however, that this checklist does not imply anyone can produce effective training material. It does require skills at knowing pace, people's learning styles and, not least, training 'tuned' communication skills.

Checklist

Requirements gathering

1 What are the objectives of the training?
  (a) There may be several objectives that need to be covered:
    (i) Business process achievement – training users to perform a new or revised business process.
    (ii) Business process administration – training users to support others performing new or revised business process.
    (iii) Systems administration – training computer operations to run the system.
    (iv) Business system overview – giving an appreciation of how the system works in the context of the business processes it is supporting.
    (v) Computer system overview – giving an appreciation of how the system is designed and how it works.
  (b) Several objectives may mean several courses although there may be some overlap, e.g. some overview elements are necessary in all courses in order to set the context for what is to follow.
  (c) Is the new system replacing an existing system?
    (i) This could be an important element in the number of training modules provided since it may need two modules to cover:
      - migrating existing-system users by indicating the differences between operating the old against operating the new
      - new users who only need to know the new.

2 What types of users exist for the system?
  (a) Draw up user profiles:
    (i) By role and system functional area (e.g. Accounts, Purchasing etc.).
    (ii) By level of responsibility (clerk, supervisor, administrator etc.).
    (iii) By frequency of use (daily, weekly, monthly, ad hoc).

(b) Allocate actual users to the various profiles.
  (i) Also note the level of IT proficiency required for the functions expected in each function.
  (ii) Cross-refer the level of IT proficiency required to the actual IT proficiency of the individuals.
(c) Note any short-falls as additional training requirements.

3 What will a user have to do outside of the system to conduct the business process?
  (a) Obtain any business process descriptions available to check for:
    (i) triggering events
    (ii) accompanying request information (i.e. forms, letters, phone calls, emails)
    (iii) non-computer-assisted tasks
    (iv) out-tray information (i.e. forms, letters, phone calls, email).
  (b) Is training required in the whole process or just the system elements? At the very least, you should cover:
    (i) data being captured by the system from forms and data added to forms by the system
    (ii) the need to understand how exceptions will be handled – what if the required data is missing from the form?

Requirements analysis

1 Draw up a matrix of training needs to be met using:
  (a) different objectives
  (b) different business processes and/or system functional areas
  (c) different user-profiles
  (d) different skill levels:
    (i) basic
    (ii) intermediary
    (iii) expert
    (iv) casual use.

2 Consolidate the matrix into the set of training modules that may be required.

3 Draw up a potential training-development plan based on:
  (a) which modules are needed 'upfront' and which modules can be deferred until later
  (b) likely length of course to achieve its objective versus user's ability to take 'time out of the business' for training. This may imply a module split.

4 Draw up how those training modules could be provided (the training approach):
  (a) There are various training mediums that could be used:
  (b) help screens in the application
  (c) training courses
  (d) presentations
  (e) self-help guidelines and manuals
  (f) computer-based training (CBT) packages
  (g) on-the-job training
  (h) individual tuition and coaching.

5   Optimize the training approach based on:
    (a)   time available for training each set of users
    (b)   suitability of the training medium to the individual (e.g. CBT may not be appropriate to low IT-literate individuals, on-the-job training may not be appropriate to the CEO)
    (c)   cost of developing the training with that module
    (d)   training lifespan:
        (i)   how frequently will the course be run?
        (ii)   how many people will need this type of training?
        (iii)   how long will we need to run this training – once? For every new recruit? Just during systems implementation (e.g. an overview may be a one-off, never-to-be repeated presentation)?

6   Present the training approach for discussion, revision and approval by the relevant management team(s).

Design (the training module and course outline)

1   Break each training module down into individual topics.

2   For each topic, draw up the specific points that need to be covered paying attention to:
    (a)   sequence
    (b)   significance (and hence time to be spent on it)
    (c)   teaching aid:
        (i)   chart/graphic
        (ii)   'bullet point' slide
        (iii)   film
        (iv)   visual aid
        (v)   exercise and feedback
        (vi)   handout
        (vii)   case study.
    (d)   Also pay close attention to any exceptions or 'special cases' that need to be handled.

3   Combine the topics into a logical sequence.

4   Check the pace of the course.
    (i)   Are the right topics covered in sufficient detail?
    (ii)   Do the topics flow appropriately?
    (iii)   Are the topic sections too long or too short? Should they be broken up or combined?

5   Walkthrough the course outline with an 'interested party' to iron out any inconsistencies.

Build

1   Now the detail of the training has been structured and designed, the training materials can actually be 'compiled'.

2   For this example, we shall assume that it is a course being built but the same can apply to the other training mediums.

3   There are a number of items that can be built into the course at this point.
   (a)   Training introduction
      (i)   Build in an introduction section to cover:
         ● instructor introduction – who I am?
         ● candidate introduction – who are you?
         ● overall structure and rules of course – start/end times, dress, comfort breaks, food/coffee breaks
         ● instructor training preferences – e.g. when interruptions are allowed
         ● layout of training location – toilets, coffee/tea facilities, catering facilities, fire exits and assembly points.
      (ii)   This may be a generic section that indicates what has to be covered but not necessarily the content (e.g. training locations will differ in their layout).
   (b)   Course overview
      (i)   What are the course objectives?
      (ii)   Who is the course aimed at and are there any precursors to the course, i.e. other courses, expected skill level, appropriate only to a specific job role etc.?
      (iii) What will people be able to do at the end of the course?
   (c)   Topic introduction
      (i)   Each topic should be introduced saying why it is there and how it fits 'the big picture'.
   (d)   Topic detail
      (i)   The topic detail needs to be fleshed out and it also needs to:
         ● include principles to apply as well as actual examples
         ● include repetition and recaps to keep reaffirming the major points
         ● include opportunities to ask questions
         ● involve people in practical work
         ● involve people in big and small group interactions.
   (e)   'Give-away' course material needs to be produced. These may include:
      (i)   handouts
      (ii)   blank exercise forms
      (iii) course book (i.e. all slides, course notes, case-study texts, bibliography, index)
      (iv)   quick-reference guide.
   (f)   Course 'giveback' material needs to be produced. This may include:
      (i)   course booking form
      (ii)   course register (e.g. completed on first day for fire-safety reasons)
      (iii) course feedback questionnaire.
   (g)   Course pace
      (i)   Based on the timings for each topic, ensure there are enough 'comfort breaks'.
      (ii)   If a course spans several days, check that the start time on the first day and the finish time on the last day are appropriate (e.g. allow people time to travel to/from training location etc.).
   (h)   Course equipment
      (i)   Depending on the various techniques employed in a course, the list of course equipment should be drawn up:
         ● overhead projector, slides, blank slides and screen (one, two or more required?)

- whiteboard(s), flipchart(s), number of pens, erasers
- video player, video projector and screen
- PC and network configuration (how many?) including OpSys, DBMS, application software
- application training environment including training user accounts and passwords, training database scripts (to load the training database with appropriate training cases).

Implementation

1   For each course to be presented, there needs to be a roll-out plan based on:

(a)   who needs the training?
(b)   how many need the training?
(c)   when do they need the training?
(d)   how many can be trained at once?
(e)   where will the training be conducted?

2   Draw up a training plan for each individual to be trained which takes into account:

(a)   how many courses an individual will require:
  - for an individual requiring many courses, the training plan will need to include sufficient 'breathing space' between courses
(b)   are there any critical dates landing in the training schedule which will affect the candidate's availability or concentration level?
  - holidays
  - business busy period (year-end, stock-taking etc.)
  - birth of a child.

3   Merge the individual training plans for each individual into a 'grand plan'.

4   Check the availability of the location(s) for the training with regard to:

(a)   training room suitability for:
  (i)   training methods (i.e. has OHP, video, computer equipment)
  (ii)   size (according to the number on the course)
  (iii)   heating/cooling and ventilation
  (iv)   hygiene factors (modern and professional looking, quiet, well lit, doesn't overlook something distracting, comfortable seating, table arrangement etc.)
  (v)   level of support (e.g. if some equipment fails what support is there for a replacement?).
(b)   training building:
  (i)   sufficient, suitable, available, nearby overnight accommodation if course is residential – sometimes this can be block booked at a discount
  (ii)   catering facilities
  (iii)   toilet facilities
  (iv)   health and safety compliant for the course numbers (including fire doors, escapes etc.).

5   Walkthrough the training plan with each individual and his/her manager to get 'sign-off'.

Maintenance

1   Training courses cannot be set in stone, they need to be monitored for maintenance.

2   Depending on the nature of the course, the monitoring period may need to be every three months, six months or annually.

3   The course needs to be changed where:
    (a)   the system has been changed:
          (i)   revised screen and/or functionality
          (ii) new screen and/or functionality
    (b)   the business process has been revised
    (c)   the course-feedback forms indicate some course deficiency
    (d)   the help desk is getting a large volume of 'nuisance calls' that could be resolved by training
    (e)   users are moving from beginner to expert
    (f)   company reorganization has changed the user base (e.g. some aspect has been outsourced).

4   Naturally, the way to maintain a course is to go back through the requirements, design and build processes to see whether the assumptions made on the way are still valid and reflect changes in the training material where they are not.

Definitions/techniques

None.

Next steps

There can be a tendency to skip the training development process in favour of 'on-the-job' training. Hence, sometimes management have to be convinced of the need for training.

Since a computer system (and business process) is only as good as the people running it, developing a training plan is a serious consideration for those who want to minimize the risk to the business of implementing a new system.

As shown above, training needs to be presented in the light of 'doing the job' and what is changing in the business not just running the computer system. On-the-job training is acceptable provided it is preceded by classroom training.

Similarly, with the best plan in the world, it still needs accomplished trainers to carry it out – staff selection in this area can be crucial. It may be that the training module designers are not necessarily the best training course presenters or training material builders. So the next step in the training plan process is to acquire the best resources to implement the plan: the trainers, the training locations etc.

8.5 Seven pillars of a service level agreement

Type: QA

Checklist description

Service Level Agreements (SLAs) have received a lot of attention since the rise of the third-party outsourcing movement. Primarily, they have been used as a guarantee between a system user and a system provider as to what each of them expects to be able to do and not do in providing and using a system.

This checklist identifies what should be covered in such an agreement. Note, however, that agreements of this nature can exist between IT departments and their internal customers as well as between separate companies providing and using software.

Checklist

User access
- Availability on-line – i.e. 8 a.m. – 6 p.m.? 24 × 7? Be careful of requesting more than required since this will push up the cost of support.
- Processing cycle for ad-hoc updates, e.g. bank tapes, cheque runs etc. – how often and what is the impact on on-line usage and response times?
- Response times (includes comms time over a LAN/WAN/Web) per transaction type:
  - simple screen refresh (e.g. enquiry screen)
  - complex screen refresh (e.g. calc running totals, bill-of-materials structure navigation etc.)
  - data save
  - complex query or search
  - simple field validation (sub second)
  - requested report.

Batch process
- Start-of-day/end-of-day processing run time (possibly by data volume).
- End-of-week, end-of-month, end-of-quarter, end-of-year processing and reports – critical items and timing.
- Deadlines for external reports (e.g. parent company cut-offs, statutory etc.).

Business benefits and volumes (especially in batch runs)
- Capacity management.
  - How much data and transactions are to be supported:
    - now
    - 6 months
    - 12 months.
  - How much overcapacity is supported in the current configuration?
  - What is the growth path if additional capacity is required?
  - Can it be invoked optionally on a needs basis and what is the lead time?
- What business benefits are we expecting to accrue?
  - Higher throughput.
  - Less rework (higher quality).

- Fewer queries and complaints.
- Fewer exceptions.
- How are the benefits to be measured?

Configuration
- Expected configuration of system – hardware, OpSys, network etc.
- What is impact on support if expected configuration changes:
  - more users
  - more servers
  - change of supplier of various system components
  - charges for assisting in the migration (including licence fees).

Role of help desk
- Minimum first-call response period:
  - for general query
  - for login and password support
  - for new user set-up
  - for software error (system still available) – possibly by transaction type
  - for system unavailable (including length of time before business suffers if no service is available).
- What response is required at what point?
  - expected average length of help-desk call
  - expected daily volume of help-desk calls
  - prioritization of calls – who determines?
  - period of 'call open' when escalation to expert is required (per type of call)
  - if a bug fix is required, how soon must it be available?
  - under what circumstances can the system be shut down for essential fix – who makes this judgement and who must they tell?
  - is there an agreed mechanism for handling 'nuisance calls' that are really a training issue?

Maintenance
- What is the agreed 'window of opportunity' for maintenance of:
  - hardware?
  - OpSys and DBMS optimization or upgrade?
  - bug-fix releases and upgrades?

Monitoring
- How will the service levels be monitored and by whom?
- Cost, penalty and impact of not meeting each service-level agreement statement. Reward and benefit sharing if SLAs are met.
- Arbitration council set-up for SLA dispute resolution.
- Review and renegotiation points
  - What are the cost options of relaxing or restricting some of the SLA requirements?
  - Can a scale be given now (plus some factoring for inflation) for different SLA options?
  - Does the agreement (including licences) cover the company for its expansion plans:
    - merger or acquisition
    - company name or status changes (e.g. flotation)

- business divestment (i.e. selling off a division)
- outsourcing of other services or systems
- growth in user base, e.g. roll-out to other departments, divisions, subsidiary companies.

Definitions/techniques

None.

Next steps

There is no point producing and signing such an agreement unless there is some intention to measure the service level. Hence the parties involved need to also create the following:

- mutually agreed measuring devices
- access by both parties to the measurements captured without 'tampering'
- assignment of individuals within both organizations whose task is to conduct measurements and report on an agreed, regular basis and to whom
- ability to conduct 'spot-check' measurements
- reporting and escalation procedure if SLA conditions are not being met
- identification of an independent party to resolve any conflicts over the interpretation of the measurements
- process for reviewing and refining SLA conditions on a regular basis (e.g. annually).

See also checklist 3.3 'Fourteen common business problems – spotting which ones are yours'.

8.6 What to look at when capacity planning

Type: Analysis

Checklist description

Sooner or later in the implementation process, the question arises as to how much physical resources to allocate and purchase to the new system. Quite often the question is orientated around the size of the database but there are many other elements to consider too.

This checklist can be used to determine what the resource requirements will be for the new system.

Checklist

Database size
- for each table, estimate table size, e.g. row width * number of rows * ((100 − fill factor)/100)
- do the same for indexes, temporary files, report files, output files
- do a projection on these figures based on percent growth per annum
- scale sizing according to archiving and housekeeping functions
- estimate size of backups and scale up according to backup and overwrite policy (e.g. seven-day retention cycle plus one-per-month etc.).

Server software size
- size of sourcecode
- size of executable (average size in memory as well as on disk)
- use of image files.

Network traffic
- how much data on average flowing between (a) server to server and (b) server to client?
- how much overhead (e.g. memory) does each connection absorb when active?
- what are the expected peaks and troughs in sessions?
- what are the hotspot time zones for establishing connections (e.g. logins at 9am, logouts at 5:30pm)?

Client software size
- size of sourcecode
- size of executable (average size in memory as well as on disk)
- use of image files.

Disaster recovery
- how much duplication and space capacity is required? Where should this be sited?

Definitions/techniques

None.

Next steps

Naturally, the output of this process may mean that further hardware may need to be purchased. On the other hand, if you have excess capacity, there may need to be a slimming down of purchase plans or investigation as to whether the spare capacity can be offered to another service.

Note that sometimes the decision with capacity management is to let the machine or application struggle since the overload is too rare and too costly to cater for.

8.7 How to do a data conversion

Type: To do

Checklist description

When converting data from one system to another, it is often difficult to know where to start. This checklist gives some ideas as to the types of problems to look out for and some of their potential solutions.

Checklist

1 Entity-level checks (target system):
   (a) Do a high-level analysis on the target system:
      (i) Identify the key entities or the entities which are 'hubs' for a number of surrounding entities – an entity group.
      (ii) Which entity groups are mandatory and what are the conditions for the existence of optional entity groups?
      (iii) Within each group, identify which entities are mandatory and which are optional. For the optional entities, what are the conditions for existence?
   (b) This analysis can be used to generate an 'attack plan' of the entity attributes to convert.
   (c) Note that some of the conditions for entities to exist may not be present in the old system – there is no data to convert and hence these entities can be ignored in the analysis.
   (d) Similarly, some mandatory entities may not have any representation in the source system – these will be dealt with below.

2 Source and target data item mapping (source to target system):
   (a) Using the 'attack plan', analyse the data items per target entity and their potential source. These will fall into various categories for conversion.
      (i) Exact data match (1:1):
         • typical cases are dates, financial, description, text
         • lookup data can be used as a direct match especially if a cross-reference table is used to convert old value to new value.
      (ii) Data with no equivalent target (1:0):
         • decisions should be made as to whether this data is to be kept
         • if it is required, a special 'historic' data table may need to be created but beware of issues of its use and maintenance – it could easily become an orphan.
      (iii) Mandatory target data with no source (0:1):
         • primary solution is to use default value to populate these fields
         • if default values cannot be used, there may be a case for marking the record as incomplete which will be completed manually in a data-cleansing exercise
         • if the data item is derived then some bulk calculator may be employed to reset the missing value. Note that it is important, where possible, to use the target systems standard calculation routines rather than invent a special one for conversion purposes.

(iv) Data to split (1:m):
- intelligent values are often candidate items for splitting – where, say, the first five letters of a code mean department and the last five mean order number
- repeating groups in the same record could also be split into several records in the new system.

(v) Data to merge (m:1):
- typically this is the case when duplicates of the same data item are to be removed or consolidated. For example, this can occur where an order and invoice data base are being merged into one system – who's got the latest customer address?
- normally most recent and timely information is most reliable
- an alternative is to look at the source which has the most reliable validations in it and use the data from that source
- need to be careful how data is matched in these situations in case there are holes in the source system's logic – how do you match invoice and order, what if delivery address is allowed to be different etc.?

(vi) Data to disperse (m:n):
- in most cases the source and target tables will be similar in structure and hence the mapping from table to table will be simple. In more complex cases the mapping will have to be derived based on:
  - what would happen under third normal form rules – i.e. data item is converted according to its relationship to the primary key, e.g. an invoice description field may be converted to a lookup code
  - business rules, e.g. a field on the target system indicates that life assurance is included in the pension – this could be transformed into a whole new data structure in the new system
  - application processing rules, e.g. the source system may have different tables for corporate customers and consumer customers – the new system may treat customers as a single entity for processing purposes.

3 Additional issues:
(a) Consider the volume of data to be converted.
   (i) How much are you taking – do you need that much?
   - can you horizontally partition the data and take it in phases (e.g. all corporate customers first then consumers)?
   - start with a small set for minor disruption and allow conversion to be short with quick success/fail result and low risk to the business.
(b) Consider special cases.
   (i) Historic data:
   - should this be converted?
   - should there be a 'balance forward' record?
   - what happens with transactions that are backdated prior to the date of conversion?
   - why not take active data only?
   (ii) Data type mismatches:
   - need to determine if this is a straightforward data-type conversion or

whether this is hiding a more complex issue, e.g. converting text or integer to money – is the source data always to two decimal places?

(iii) Interpretation of derived data:
- does 'balance' in the old system mean exactly the same in the new system?
- it may be safer to recalculate all derived data items afresh in the new system to prevent 'interpretation' problems.

(iv) Low-value data:
- certain collections of data may not be worth the trouble of converting, e.g. customers of 10 years ago who have still not paid their final balance of £20
- need to decide what is economical to convert
- this is especially true of data that has been carried forward from new system to new system and is now extremely old. Typically, this type of data will give the most problems in conversion since it was added when the source system was at its newest and hence more bug ridden.

(v) 'Dirty data' domains:
- do not assume that the source data is within the tolerances specified – it should be analysed for domain integrity
- all data fields for conversion should be tested to ensure that they conform to the rules that will be expected by the new system
- for some examples:
  - ensure that what is assumed to be mandatory data in the source system is actually present in all records etc.
  - integers or floats contain no negatives that they aren't supposed to or any other 'out-of-bounds' value
  - values like 999999999.99 should be treated with caution
  - check the format of 'common' fields, e.g. telephone numbers can be '01999 123456' or '(01999) 123456 ext 22'. Similarly with the format of dates, sortcodes etc.
- need to compare the source domain with the target domain and what to do about 'dirty data' domain occurrences in the source data – typically clean them before conversion.

(c) Check that the system is covered by company's current Data Protection Act registration and re-register if not.

Definitions/techniques

Third normal form – see checklist 5.11 'How to do a data modelling'.

Domain integrity – most data items have a data type, e.g. character, integer, float, but also have a domain, telephone number, postcode. A domain is a set of generic rules about how that data item will behave or be formatted.

Next steps

Produce a data mapping systems design document.

Note that almost all systems contain data that is incorrect, incomplete or out of date. 'Dirty data' is often the result of the old system's peculiarities including bugs and erroneous defaults. Companies often take the opportunity to fix this data in the implementation of a new system.

This is acceptable, but it is easy to overload an already busy implementation schedule with the extra burden of cleaning data not just converting it. Sometimes it is better to separate the two exercises – either cleaning it up on the old system before it is converted or cleaning it up on the new system after it has been converted.

8.8   Nine important documents to hand over from development to the support team

Type: QA

Checklist description

Quite often, a system is built and installed by a development team, and the support team then have to 'pick it up and run with it'. This approach, however, has a number of drawbacks:

- Knowledge essential to the 'well-being' of the system often fails to be communicated – putting the implementation, and hence the business, at risk.
- Support team are demotivated when they cannot confidently respond to the actual users of the system.
- Business users become unconfident in the support team's ability to handle the system and this can have a negative effect on the system's usage.
- Development staff get involved in support issues and get 'locked in' to supporting systems when they'd rather be developing the next one.

In order to successfully handover a system from development to the support team, this checklist identifies what items should also be made available and what they can be used for.

Checklist

Project Charter
The charter should include the raison d'être for the project which will assist the support team in recognizing fundamental support issues – what is the key to the success of this project or implementation? What key areas must we support?

Business Requirement Specifications
Should any queries arise regarding whether a particular function is in error or is as specified, the Business Requirement Specifications must be consulted to determine whether the support team or development must be involved. Also, certain statistics such as expected volumes etc. would be required to monitor required vs actual performance.

System Specification
Since the support team will be making program changes it is important that the design specifications are available so that the impact of any bugs reported can be traced and potential solutions identified.

Technical Specification and Limitations
It is required that the operating environment be identified including memory and disk-space requirements, what speed processor etc. so that appropriate hardware or software can be configured.

Operator Manual including Restart/Recovery
What is expected in terms of backups, daily, weekly, monthly cycles etc.? What should be done when errors occur. How should new software or bug fixes be released?

Organization chart including lists of legal users and roles and responsibilities

The sponsor, the senior users, the system 'expert' and who is responsible for what aspect of the system should be identified and agreed so that as queries arise the relevant parties can be notified or consulted.

Training Plan for Support Staff

As with any handover, there should be a handover training exercise to transfer the knowledge from the development staff to the support staff.

Implementation Plan

All aspects of the implementation should be planned – the installation of hardware and software, conversion of existing data or population of the new database etc.

Contingency or Disaster Recovery Plan

Depending on how critical the system is to the business (as defined in the Project Charter), there may need to be contingency plans should there be fire or theft. The support team will need to have a 'ready to go' plan if these circumstances ever arise.

Definitions/techniques

None.

Next steps

These items should be produced by the development or implementation teams prior to the handover of the system to the support team. Each item should be checked that it contains the required information.

In practice, it is often difficult to refuse the delivery of a system. However, it is worth stressing the risk to the business if you do not have sufficient information on which to maintain the system – if only to cover your back.

8.9   Assessing the long-term viability of a system

Type: Analysis

Checklist description

The following is a checklist of areas to be used in assessing the long-term support viability of an application. It can be used for both in-house and external developments or packages and may also be applied to technical options.

It should be noted that not all systems are expected to have a long 'shelf-life' – this should be determined as part of the Project Charter and these tests applied in the light of that expectation.

This list could be turned into a score sheet to give an overall scoring and presented on a star chart.

Checklist

Architecture design
- Is the system architecturally sound? Does it fit in with the long-term IT application and technical strategies or is it a workaround or stop-gap?
- Does the system provide a growth path or is it fundamentally limiting (unless reworked)?
- Will it become overburdened with requests for change which cannot be supported by its internal design?
- How many systems does it interface with? Is the system supporting several other systems? Is the system supported by several other systems? Are these systems internal or external to the company?
- Is the level of change in these systems within an organization's control or controlled by outside forces?
- How complex is the architecture which the system is supporting? Is it deeply embedded in a network of systems? Is it part of a chain of systems/business processes? Is it stand-alone?
- How much knowledge of these other systems will be required to support this system?

Build quality
- IIas the system been developed with the proper use of standards (e.g. code standards, program naming, data naming, project lifecycle etc.)?
- Has the KISS principle been applied? Are all the modules obvious in what they do and they do only one thing?
- Is it obvious how the programs fit together?
- Is the system built using standard tools – operating systems, languages and databases? Do upgrades in these components create a high or low level of rework of the system? Can the system be kept up to date in terms of its technical environment at little or no cost?
- Does the code contain obscure system, language functions or make use of loopholes in existing databases, languages, compilers or operating systems?
- If the system is primarily package based, does upgrading the package create a high/low level of rework for the system? Has the package been tailored to make the interface easier?
- Is the system and all of its components, tools and environments year 2000 compliant?

Business/technical change

- Does the system allow for growth and business change by the use of parameters or is everything 'hard coded'?
- How sensitive is the system to changes in business practices, organizational structure, commercial environment (e.g. base rate changes), legal/statutory requirements? Are changes in these areas merely parameter changes or more fundamental recoding changes?
- How much change is expected, planned and designed for in terms of size (database and storage), throughput (number of queries and transactions), usage (number of users)? What is the maximum allowed by the system? What is the safe or most-comfortable limit? What limits have been tested?
- How close to the safe or comfortable limit is the system going to run (from day 1)?
- Can the system keep step with upgrades in technical platforms – hardware, operating system, database, compiler, language standards?

Support mechanisms (error and recovery)

- Does the system contain both error checking and error handling? What errors have been anticipated? What errors have not been anticipated?
- Does the system contain an audit trail or program/transaction log that can be used to identify errors have occurred and assist in tracking down where an error has originated from? Are the error messages helpful for fault diagnosis?
- Is the system backed up? Is this automatic? What does the backup include – data? environment? programs? Has the backed-up system ever been fully restored and shown to work (including a test to prove no loss or truncation of data)? How quickly can the system be restored?
- Does the system have a recovery mechanism that can be activated? How complex is it to recover? In what circumstances can the recovery mechanism be activated? What situations are not covered? Does the recovery mechanism depend on other recovery systems? Is it tied to a chain of recovery activities?
- Is there a natural time window for maintenance, support and recovery activities? Does this fit in with business system-availability targets?
- What recovery scenarios have been anticipated and tested?
- Is there a disaster-recovery, business-contingency and fallback plan in case of failure? Is it viable? Has it been tested?
- How easy it is to reproduce and test bugs? Can the production environment be duplicated for testing?
- Does it have a performance monitor and how accurate is it?
- What other support mechanisms have been built in? Are there any other built-in diagnostics or checking tools (e.g. use of checksum or separate data-integrity checking tools)? Is there a procedure to run regular checks?

Internal knowledge

- Does the system require 'expert' knowledge in order to diagnose faults if they occur?
- How easy is it to transfer knowledge of the system between support staff? Has it been done? How long does it take to become a competent support person?
- What skills and knowledge would a potential support person need to have already before being trained in the system (and to what degree)? Are these skills readily available in the marketplace? Is the pool of relevant skills declining or increasing?

- How many staff have the required skills/knowledge? How many staff have experience with the system from a support point of view?
- Does the system contain its own help?
- Has the system been adequately documented (i.e. requirement document, data and process design documents, operator's guide including environment build specifications and recovery system guide, user guide)? Are the documents complete, up to date, accurate? Have the documents been used by non-authors – especially environment build specifications, operator's user guide and recovery system user guide?
- Is there some fault-diagnosis document, charts, diagrams and lists? Are all the error messages described in terms of cause/effect and resolution? Is this document published and available to support staff?
- Is there a method to add to the fault-diagnosis document so that knowledge of errors and recoveries is improved and shared?

Support organization

- How much support is expected or needed? Can the system be 'temperamental' depending on volumes and/or other processes running on the same machine? Does the system depend on other processes which may hang or abort (e.g. telecommunications)?
- How automated is the system? Does it need constant action and monitoring on the part of an operator? Has it got an hourly, daily, weekly, monthly cycle which requires manual action or intervention (e.g. setting of system dates, logicals etc.)?
- Is it clear who is responsible for which component in the system – i.e. who is responsible for operating and/or using the system? Does this include monitoring for errors? Who do they notify of an error? Who prepares and recommends the recovery action? Who must see and review it? Who must approve it? Who must do it?
- Is there a known 'first-port-of-call' for any errors that occur?
- Is there a known and used escalation cycle for problems?
- Does the escalation cycle need to include an external resource, i.e. outside of the company's control? What is their response time? Does it conform to contract? Is it as per company's needs and business continuity?
- Can new errors and recoveries be documented so that they can be used by others?
- Is the support organization external and has it got a long-term future? Are there any alternatives to this organization?

Definitions/techniques

KISS – Keep It Simple, Stupid – the golden rule for all systems designs.

Next steps

It's always good to 'look before you leap' when taking on new systems either homegrown or bought-in packages.

If there are question marks about the long-term support of a system, it may be that the system is not worth the investment so either find a system that is or seek to negotiate the cost of the system downwards.

Inevitably, however, all systems have a limited lifespan – see checklist 8.10 'After implementation – living with the system'.

8.10 After implementation – living with the system

Type: Analysis

Checklist description

What with all the pain involved in developing and implementing a system, there is the temptation to just sit back and be satisfied 'once it's in'. However, it's important to take the long-term view of a system. Why? Because systems get old. As the business grows and develops, a static system struggles to keep up. Over time, the system, designed some time ago, will become less and less applicable to the business as it is now.

Checklist

Recognize its lifespan
- Creation – initial, unstable.
- Development – expanding rapidly but not there yet.
- Maturity – running smoothly, stable.
- Decline – struggling to maintain pace.
- Death – retirement.

Recognize what affects its lifespan
- Changes in technology (affects staffing).
- Changes in vendor status.
- Changes in business environment/strategy.
- Level of previous maintenance/investment.

How do you spot an out-of-date system?
- Many workarounds and manual procedures to system use.
- Using the system is not intuitive compared to the business process.
- Large maintenance bill with little improvement.
- Same system can now be bought as a package with more features.
- Hardware/software platform that the system depends on is no longer supported nor widely in use.
- Hardware/software platform that the system depends on has no upgrade path.
- Difficult to recruit IT staff who want to work on that hardware/software platform.

Definitions/techniques

None.

Next steps

See also checklist 8.9 'Assessing the long-term viability of a system'.

8.11 Questions to ask at the post-implementation review

Type: To do

Checklist description

This is a simple checklist intended to assist in a post-implementation review. The chief aim of which is not to apportion blame nor to grab the credit. The chief aim is to help in the next project.

Checklist

1   What were the original goals and how close did we get to achieving them?

2   Where did we fail and what was the reason for failure?

3   How could we avoid that failure in future?

4   Did we use any good problem-solving techniques? Did we use any unproductive ones?

5   How good was the development technique? What could have been done better and how? What could be dispensed with since it didn't add any value?

6   How on time and on budget were we? Can we revise the function-point estimates we used to generate the estimates for this project?

Definitions/techniques

None.

Next steps

Since the main aim of this exercise is to feed back into the next project, there needs to be a project-experience book or checklist that should be used to record the outcome of this review. This book or checklist is a central resource added to by each and every project.

This project-experience book should be the first document that all project managers use at the start of a new project – see checklist 1.2 'Five key areas to understand when starting a project'.

Printed and bound by CPI Group (UK) Ltd, Croydon, CR0 4YY

17/10/2024

01775697-0005